PREVENTING READING FAILURE

Books by Jeannette Jansky and Katrina de Hirsch

PREVENTING READING FAILURE

PREDICTING READING FAILURE

Paul B. Hoeber (Cashed check)

PREVENTING

READING

FAILURE

Prediction, Diagnosis, Intervention

JEANNETTE JANSKY

KATRINA DE HIRSCH

1817

HARPER & ROW, PUBLISHERS
New York, Evanston, San Francisco, London

FIRST EDITION

STANDARD BOOK NUMBER: 06–012171–8

LIBRARY OF CONGRESS CATALOG CARD NUMBER: 72–79674

Contents

Foreword

In 1969 a Task Force on Dyslexia and Related Reading Disorders of the U.S. Department of Health, Education, and Welfare issued a report highlighting the unbelievable magnitude of the country's educational crisis. It pointed out that in our complex industrialized society reading failure represents a lifetime disability for the individual and a major impediment to social progress.

The report further noted a paucity of solid data regarding the detection and remediation of reading disabilities, and, more particularly, the lack of any organized study of the "strategies" whereby, within a given school, children with reading disabilities could systematically be identified and treated. In general, current practice is to enter children in school at some standard age to provide regular instruction and, if the child fails, to require him to repeat a grade until he has mastered the skills necessary for advanced study. In some schools he is pushed ahead, regardless. The committee concluded that across the country there are few schools that have developed a systematic and consistent approach to the remediation of reading failure, and even fewer that have addressed themselves to prevention.

A problem of this magnitude and national significance cannot be dealt with on a hit-or-miss basis. The inadequacy of present approaches is evident from the national figures. It will yield only if every school system has a well-developed program for *prevention*. This more hopeful approach is based upon the reasonable assumption that children differ in their cognitive characteristics, and that a method of teaching which is effective for most children will not necessarily be the best for all. It further assumes that characteristics which lead to failure in reading can be recognized *before* the child is subjected to psychological trauma and that appropriate intervention at an early time can prevent such failure.

The application of this principle demands a program within each school system that evaluates children sometime *before* they enter the first grade, with the aim of identifying those who are destined to fail and of providing them with tools that will allow them to cope. The need, therefore, is for tests designed to detect children requiring special intervention as well as methods of intervention appropriate to each child's constellation of disabilities.

Jansky and de Hirsch have addressed themselves to each of these steps. Their major contribution has been the development of a several-stage screening method for the preschool prediction of reading failure in large populations. While this screening method predicts for individual children, administration requires a minimum of time and can be taught to teachers and paraprofessionals. Within the representative population that Jansky studied, her instrument designated 76 to 83 percent of those children who subsequently failed in reading (which in her group varied from 14 to 63 percent). Considering the inevitable variations in teaching methods, which must have significantly influenced children's subsequent achievement, this is a remarkable accomplishment.

One important concept developed from these studies is that from a practical point of view the cutoff point used as a basis for a pass-fail prediction should be adapted to each school and to the socioeconomic background of the group being tested.

Other efforts at prediction may have failed to achieve wide acceptance because they did not recognize this variable.

The screening procedure also differs from many others in its heavy emphasis on language development and linguistic abilities as opposed to the simple perceptuo-motor aspects of neural development.

This report is almost unique, moreover, in its emphasis on the *strategy* of intervention. It provides a blueprint for a total program for early recognition and diagnosis of reading disability. The authors start with the assumption that the ability to read rests on a large variety of factors operating in the child's earliest years, and they discuss the rationale behind the various existing programs that deal with prevention of learning disabilities long before the child is exposed to formal education. It is evident that there are innumerable practical problems to be resolved and that it is essential to ascertain the social and economic costs of preventive as opposed to remedial programs. The answer to this question is clearly of the utmost practical significance and deserves to be carefully explored. The present book is an important step in that direction.

RICHARD MASLAND
Moses Professor and Chairman,
Department of Neurology,
Columbia University

Acknowledgments

This book owes a great deal to a great many.

Its primary concern is a comprehensive plan for prediction and diagnosis of subsequent reading problems. The test batteries developed were the product of a longitudinal study that was supported, at a time when funds were scarce, by a generous grant from the Health Research Council of the City of New York. Dr. Edward Curnen's support throughout and his sponsorship in obtaining some assistance from the Babies Hospital Fund were essential for completion of the task. The Aaron Norman Foundation's financial assistance was deeply appreciated. Mrs. Augusta Lyons' help at a particularly difficult moment will not be forgotten. Barbara and Gerald Goldsmith have long been interested in the subject of this book and have also contributed to the undertaking.

The diagnostic battery grew out of research for a doctoral dissertation. The emphasis in the original research was different, but the guidance of the Dissertation Committee was extremely helpful. Professor Anne McKillop was chairman of the committee and Professors Miriam Goldberg and Walter MacGinitie were the other members.

Curtis Jansky spent many hours writing computer programs

for various aspects of the predictive study. He was invariably ready to help, and his help was crucial.

The enthusiasm, reliability, and skill of the examiners accounted in large part for the quality of the data. Mrs. Russel Beatie, Mrs. Marion Carr, Mrs. Anton Coppola, Mrs. Lazlo de Mandy, and Mrs. James Tower participated in both phases of testing. Mrs. Fidelio Bonito, Mrs. George Harris, and Mrs. Frederick Hurd ably assisted.

Mrs. Anton Coppola's care in transcribing the children's stories and Mrs. Geza Gazdag's assistance in judging them were appreciated.

Participating district superintendents and school principals could hardly have been more cooperative. For school personnel our presence meant interruption in already busy schedules and incursion into precious space. The principals' and teachers' comments about the children were invaluable and revealed how much they care. We had an entertaining time with many of the five hundred children who participated in the study. Their faces and varied styles are a memorable part of this phase of the work.

The introductory chapter of this book is a considerably modified version of a preliminary report written by the Task Force on Prediction for the Interdisciplinary Committee on Reading Problems. Its chairman, Dr. Archie Silver, an old friend, and Dr. Alfred Hayes had many useful suggestions. The chapter owes a debt to three of the committee members, Dr. Richard Masland, Dr. Robert Dykstra, and Dr. Albert Harris for the critical reading of the earlier manuscript.

The last chapter grew out of a background paper written for the National Advisory Committee on Dyslexia and Related Reading Disorders. Some of the material was published by the National Institute of Neurological Disease and Stroke in *Reading Forum* in 1971.

The authors are grateful to Dr. William Langford, whose

interest in language disorders, which goes back over thirty years, has given them a chance to engage in the clinical research which ultimately forms the basis for this study.

Mary Pockman's editorial assistance has been valuable.

JEANNETTE JANSKY
KATRINA DE HIRSCH

Introduction

"As many as 18.5 million Americans . . . lack the reading ability necessary for survival in the United States today," according to the National Reading Council (Brezeinski and Howard, 1971). This figure represents more than 10 percent of the population, and it is obvious that the problem deserves serious and urgent consideration on the national level. However, the absence of a national policy has resulted in haphazard and fragmented approaches to the problem.

This book represents an attempt to prevent reading failure. It is unlikely that such failure can be totally eliminated. Like sin, it will be with us always. But we believe that a very early attack on reading problems will prevent failure in a large number of children, including those whose life circumstances do not foster an involvement with printed words.

Prevention involves three steps: preschool identification of children likely to fail; diagnostic assessment of such children; and appropriate intervention. At present, the final step, remediation, is often initiated only after the child has fallen far behind, after his self-image has been severely damaged and his sense of failure has spilled over into other learning experiences. The result is a sweeping rejection of all educational goals.

There is need for an early epidemiological approach, which

usually implies testing of children in groups and reliance on means and standard deviations. But reading is a complex phenomenon, and children are complex organisms. In group testing, the individual child's specific approach to problem solving is totally lost.

The approach presented here is epidemiological. However, it utilizes a test battery which is not only suitable for screening large groups of children but is also so short that it permits children to be tested individually.

The first chapter is an overview of approaches to prediction and their pitfalls. It discusses theoretical issues and redefines the task in the light of current needs.

The second chapter presents a broad blueprint for identification of high-risk children. This plan integrates subjective data with test scores so as to provide a comprehensive picture of the individual's functioning. The plan also suggests a method for tailoring norms to the academic demands of particular schools.

Chapter 3 is concerned with the diagnostic assessment of children singled out by a screening process as prospective failing readers. The focus of diagnosis as proposed here is not upon performance based on a desultory, haphazard collection of single tests but rather on competences that underlie these tests. An analysis of deficits and strengths in these competences, supplemented by subjective judgment of a child's maturity and his attitude toward learning, yields a profile of his functioning and provides essential leads for intervention.

Problems of prediction and diagnosis are illustrated by case presentations in Chapter 4.

The last chapter deals with intervention. It examines the rationales underlying existing programs and recommends a radical approach to intervention. Now being tried out in a few isolated experimental centers, this approach stresses the necessity for the earliest possible action, heavy parental involvement, and the fusing of cognitive and affective aspects of learning.

CHAPTER I

Approaches to Prediction[1]

KATRINA DE HIRSCH, SHIRLEY FELDMANN, FLORENCE ROSWELL

Severe difficulties with reading cut the individual adrift from the cultural mainstream and constitute formidable obstacles to his economic and social survival. In the presence of massive reading and spelling difficulties, the prevailing response of the schools has been to begin remedial intervention after problems are clearly established, too late to prevent crippling emotional disturbances and the snowballing social costs of reading failure.

We can no longer afford to wait until children are in trouble. If intervention is to be timely and effective, it is imperative to identify potentially failing readers at the earliest possible age. This is the purpose of the predictive and diagnostic instruments to be presented in this book.

When children are first exposed to formal reading instruction, they respond in a total fashion. Their responses are determined by a number of factors, including psychobiological endowment, early life experiences, sociocultural milieu, the

---

1. A different version of this paper was originally prepared for the Interdisciplinary Committee on Reading Problems. The senior author was the chairman of the Task Force on Prediction. The other members were Robert Dykstra, Richard Masland, William Stokoe, Thomas Barrett, and Robert D. Hess. All of them read the original (unpublished) manuscript and gave most helpful criticism. The present paper uses some of the material of the early version.

school situation, and the complex interrelationships among all of these variables. It would be desirable to explore the *interaction* of the multivariate forces that converge on the child and that determine his response to early education. Predictive studies have not, however, arrived at this degree of sophistication. What they have tried to do is either to identify *single* aspects of functioning which may be predictively linked to reading success or failure or to investigate *combinations* of variables and explore their association with subsequent achievement.

Most predictive studies use correlation techniques to demonstrate the relationship between early testing and later performance. These techniques allow only for probability statements and are sometimes wrongly assumed to imply causality.

The following review of approaches to prediction first discusses the association with subsequent reading scores of a number of *single* variables: chronological age; sex; intelligence; socioeconomic factors; neurological status; laterality; visual perception; body image; visuomotor competence; auditory perception; oral language, intersensory integration, and emotional status. It then turns to predictive instruments based on *combinations* of variables. These include reading readiness tests, predictive batteries, and teachers' assessments. The review is not intended to be a "state of the art" presentation; neither is it a summary of the major approaches to prediction. Individual studies considered pertinent to the discussion are included for purposes of illustration. Finally, some of the general problems involved in prediction will be taken up.

Prediction from Single Variables

Discussing the predictive usefulness of single variables in no way implies that reading difficulties stem from single perceptual, linguistic, cognitive, social, or personality characteristics. We hope to demonstrate that reading disorders are always related to constellations of dysfunctions and environmental factors, and that the interaction between them varies from child to child. The authors agree with Lambert (1967) that investigations into academic effectiveness, or lack of it, should emphasize a multivariate rather than a single-variable design.

CHRONOLOGICAL AGE AND SEX

Chronological age was the criterion for first-grade admission in 68 percent of schools included in the Harvard Report on Reading in Elementary Schools (Austin and Morrison, 1963).

Chall (1967) has described how the political climate and the temper of the times influence thinking about the optimal age for beginning reading instruction. An example is the general outcry for earlier academic achievement after the advent of Sputnik.

The timing of exposure to early education is an expression of the social structure and philosophy of a given historical period. When children were considered to be small replicas of adults, cognitive development and acquisition of literary skills (reserved for a small segment of society) were encouraged at the earliest possible age. This point of view no longer prevails. Today we see a degree of variability from country to country and even within the same national community as to the most appropriate age for exposure to printed words. In Scotland children begin to learn letters and sounds when they are five years old. Swedish youngsters enter first grade at the age of seven.

In the United States there was a trend toward earlier school admission between 1918 and 1957. After 1957 the trend was reversed. Today educators generally assume that by the time a child reaches the age of five to seven his perceptuomotor, cognitive, social, and emotional development will enable him to cope with reading; they believe, thus, that chronological age at first-grade entrance is a moderately good predictor of performance in the elementary grades. In a broad sense they are right. Most children who enter school at around the age of six are ready to learn to read, a finding that is consistent with Piaget's (1952) and Gesell's thesis (1940) that for the most part chronological age reflects neurophysiological and cognitive maturation.

It has never been doubted that certain children are ready for printed words long before the age of six (Durkin, 1966; Sutton, 1969). On the other hand, there are those whose age and intellectual potential would entitle them to first-grade entrance but who do not respond, the children described by Ilg and Ames (1965) as "superior immatures." For both groups chronological age alone is a poor predictor.

It is possible that chronological age at first-grade entrance should be viewed in relation to sex.[2] Among the "superior immatures," the majority are boys. Most studies report that girls are ready to read earlier than are boys and that they retain this advantage through the lower grades. Stanchfield (1971) found poorer listening habits and greater difficulty with auditory discrimination in boys. Whether these differences are culturally determined, whether they are related to psychodynamic factors, or whether they result from the slower maturational rhythm of boys has not been resolved. Tanner (1961) commented on the fact that around the age of six, boys lag twelve months behind girls in skeletal age.

In his intensive readiness study based on Swedish pupils, Johansson (1965) found that younger children were generally less ready and able to work than were older ones; the lag in readiness was far greater in the case of boys. In Jansky's investigation (Chapters 2 and 4) age was important for success in the case of white girls: Only four of the forty *older* white girls failed in

2. That chronological age is a poor predictor is surprising to clinicians who find that younger children are at a disadvantage. De Hirsch, Jansky, *et al.* (1966) found that those kindergarten tests that were most sensitive to age changes were the best predictors. It is, of course, possible that the weak or negative correlations between chronological age and reading achievement are influenced by the fact that some school systems permit only very bright and mature youngsters to enter first grade at early ages.

reading at the end of second grade. In the light of these findings, the question of whether age at first-grade entrance should differ for boys and girls takes on new significance.

Predictions in general are considerably more stable for girls than for boys. Kagan's investigation (1969) dealing with babies between the ages of four and fourteen months is a case in point. When Goffeney et al. (1971) studied Bayley scores of eight-month-old babies, he found that among girls mental and fine motor scores correlated significantly with WISC IQs and with Bender Gestalt scores at age eight. In the study by de Hirsch, Jansky, et al. (1966), fourteen out of nineteen tests showed higher correlations with subsequent reading in the case of girls.

Durrell (1958), Barrett (1965b), and Dykstra (1966) also found chronological age wanting as a predictor. Their results indicate that a study of the interaction between age and sex might be enlightening. Singer et al. (1968) suggest that different tests or perhaps different scoring systems may be needed for boys and for girls.

INTELLIGENCE AND SOCIOECONOMIC STATUS

Educators have long believed that a child's intelligence is a crucial factor in determining readiness. It should be emphasized that in this context the word *intelligence* stands for a score on an intelligence measure. Such measurements sample a wide variety of competences and probably represent some unknown and subtle interaction between environment and potential.

With the growing enthusiasm for intelligence testing in the early thirties, a number of workers began to investigate the usefulness of IQ scores for assessing first-grade readiness. Mental age became the yardstick for determining the optimal age for beginning reading instruction. Morphett and Washburne (1931) were responsible for the long-accepted belief that an MA of 6.5 years was desirable. Others maintain that children with MAs of 5 years would be capable of learning to read. Correlations between MA and reading scores are reported to range from .43 to .75.

It is, of course, well known that reading disabilities occur on all intellectual levels. In a fair number of cases we find discrepancies between performance on reading readiness tests and intelligence evaluations. Educators are therefore no longer so optimistic about the validity of IQ as a predictor in the early grades. In the higher grades, on the other hand, when the reading task demands more advanced linguistic and cognitive competences, verbal intelligence test scores become far better predictors of reading achievement. Fransella and Gerber (1965) reported that the correlation between reading age and scores on the verbal section of the WISC increases with chronological age. The high correlation between the two measures may, of course, represent an overlapping of competences, and the pertinent question arises to what degree they evaluate similar dimensions. Vygotsky (1962) postulates that the association between language (in this case printed language) and thought becomes much closer as children grow older.

It should be stressed that the intelligence test scores of deprived children are rarely meaningful. To a considerable extent, these scores reflect the richness of the child's milieu and how much he has benefited from it. Haywood (1967) states that IQ scores measure the interaction between genetic endowment and conditions of rearing. Furthermore, children from deprived backgrounds are not test oriented, and they are often unfamiliar with the examiner's style of communication. Thus, intelligence tests may well predict that these children will fail to learn to read—and they will often be right, because the tests are, in fact, good predictors. What is much less certain is their usefulness for evaluating potential.[3] Predictive instruments

3. Montagu (1971) speaks about "social malnutrition" resulting from exposure to inadequate, ambiguous, and confusing stimuli in the earliest years which prevents some children from realizing their genetic potential.

have similar drawbacks. Weiner and Feldmann (1950) administered their Reading Prognosis Test to lower and middle class populations and found a significant relationship between socioeconomic status and test scores. They believe that conventional prognostic instruments do not yield interpretable scores for children from lower social levels. The content, format, and methods of existing tests (Feldmann, 1967–68) are replete with words, concepts, and experiences foreign to the world of deprived children. Thus, social class is a crucial factor in children's test performance.

The usual indicators of socioeconomic status (parental educational attainment, income, and occupation) are useful but only *gross* variables, statements of probability that children will encounter certain experiences (Hess and Shipman, 1965). Stodolsky and Lesser (1967) rightly plead for a more refined assessment of environment insisting that the "culturally deprived" group is not homogeneous but encompasses wide variations. There is clearly a need to identify the specific socioeconomic and cultural factors which might be useful as early predictors of reading success or failure.

Children are exposed to distinct patterns of learning long before they start their formal education. Learning is mediated through the social group and the life-style of children from deprived backgrounds is hardly conducive to coping with formal instruction. Birch and Belmont (1965b), for example, say that even at very early ages socioeconomic differences are associated with differences in relatively simple perceptual functions which are basic to cognition. Hess and his co-workers explored early mother-child interaction and demonstrated its importance for subsequent cognitive development. They showed that the child's performance on cognitive tasks is associated with the "teaching style" of the mother, whom they viewed as a programmer of input during the preschool years; this association is as close as or closer than the associations with such measures as maternal IQ or "social class." The mother's "teaching style," thus, is a useful predictor variable independent of socioeconomic status.

Learning handicaps are particularly glaring in children from deprived backgrounds where English, if it is spoken at all, is spoken as a foreign language. Such children start school with linguistic handicaps, often compounded by a background of experiences and values which differ radically from those of their English-speaking peers.

Predictive instruments suitable for Spanish-speaking children are practically nonexistent. We do not know whether their lags are related to their limited knowledge of English, or to cultural differences, or to interaction between the two. Puerto Ricans, for example, seem to differ from other groups in their less verbal response (Stodolsky and Lesser, 1967).

It is by no means clear, furthermore, whether predictions are equally stable for deprived and for middle class youngsters. Weiner and Feldmann (1950) as well as Jansky (Chapter 2) found that predictions did hold up for lower class children, perhaps because the vicissitudes of life in the slums constitute as much of an "expected environment" as that of middle class youngsters.

In summary, it is imperative that predictive studies be explicit about their assumptions regarding the relationship between intelligence, socioeconomic status, and learning. The interaction among them cannot be explored before these variables are carefully defined. In any case, generalizations from the data must be limited in keeping with the nature of the sample.

NEUROLOGICAL STATUS

A good deal of discussion has centered around the use of early neurological status as a possible predictor of subsequent reading performance.[4]

4. The authors are indebted to Dr. Richard Masland for many of the formulations in this section.

A retrospective study by Kawi and Pasamanick (1958) com-pared the histories of children with reading disabilities to those of controls matched by age, sex, and mother's age at birth. When prematurity, complications of pregnancy and labor, and difficulties during the neonatal period were all taken into con-sideration, 45 percent of the children with reading disabilities were found to have been exposed to one or more complications, in contrast to 28 percent of the controls (a difference significant at the .05 level of confidence).

Although such difference suggests that early brain injury may be implicated in reading disability, Masland (1968) points out that the association with reading is not necessarily a direct one. According to him, brain injury may result in a variety of dysfunctions including gross intellectual impair-ment, behavior disorders, disturbances of sensory and motor functions, and severe language deficits, depending on the ex-tent of the injury, the areas of the brain involved, and the age at which the insult occurs. A verifiable history of brain injury[5] and positive signs on the classic neurological exami-nation may give rise to the suspicion of an associated impair-ment of the neurological functions underlying language and reading skills, but the association between cerebral involve-ment and reading is indirect.

The term *minimal brain injury* is frequently mentioned in connection with reading disability. There are reservations as to the use of this term, mainly because the diagnosis is an inferen-tial one and the definition of the term varies from one clinical setting to another. Clinical evidence, however, does seem to indicate that "soft" neurological signs—that is, a variety of dys-

5. It might be useful to list some factors which could result in brain injury and thus heighten the risk of possible subsequent reading disorder: hypertension, toxemia, eclampsia, and hemorrhage in the prenatal phase; neonatal jaundice, severe birth trauma, asphyxia, and prematurity in the perinatal; and convul-sions, feeding difficulties, failure to thrive, and delay in neurological develop-ment in the neonatal period. Lyle (1970), in a retrospective study, found that a combination of birth injury, epileptiform symptoms, and speech defects best predicted difficulties with verbal learning.

functions such as motility disturbances, perceptuomotor deficits, trouble with abstract functioning—are frequent concomitants of reading disability.

If, as suggested by Bender (1958), cerebral dysfunction manifests itself primarily through interference with maturational processes, then some aspects of cerebral dysfunction might be measured indirectly by assessing lags in central nervous system organization.

The collaborative perinatal study supported by the National Institute of Neurological Disease and Stroke may help to clarify the predictive relationship between impaired neurological integrity at early ages and subsequent reading disorders. Exact and complete data regarding the circumstances of prenatal and perinatal development are available for some fifty thousand children between the ages of two and eight years. A continuing evaluation of the reading competence of this group of children would provide highly significant information as to the association between neurological dysfunction and reading failure in the elementary grades.

LATERALITY

That the neurological organization corresponding to left cerebral dominance is basic to verbal symbolic behavior has been corroborated by Kimura's experiments (1961) in dichotic listening. This work demonstrates that verbal symbolic material (speech) is processed in the left cerebral hemisphere, while nonverbal information (environmental noises, animal sounds, clicks, and so on) is by and large processed by the right one. Cerebral dominance might be pertinent for reading inasmuch as reading is a verbal activity (Liberman, 1971). Orton's hypothesis (1937) that lack of cerebral dominance gives rise to a variety of language disturbances thus acquires new meaning. His assumption that handedness reflects cortical dominance has, however, been challenged.[6] The fact is, we do not know.

As far back as 1935, Monroe questioned the assumption that ambiguous lateralization at kindergarten age is necessarily a precursor of reading disability. Ambiguous lateralization between the age of five and six, according to de Hirsch, Jansky, *et al.* (1966), did not preclude adequate reading competence at the end of the second grade. Birch and Belmont (1965a) reported that crossed laterality patterns and ambilaterality did not discriminate between competent and failing readers in the higher grades.

Lateralization is probably also a matter of maturation. Most young children are ambidextrous. Subirana (1961) found that the EEGs of strongly right-handed youngsters are more mature than those of ambidextrous ones. Thus, the hypothetical relationship between poor reading and ambilaterality may rest on an underlying maturational dysfunction common to both.

Birch and Belmont (1965a) found that lack of awareness between right and left characterized retarded readers. The question is complicated by the fact that no one really knows what is involved in right-left awareness. Benton (1968) makes the important point that right-left awareness is a complex phenomenon involving both somatosensory components—the right-left gradient body schema—and a linguistic symbolic component. Conceptualizations have emphasized the former and neglected the latter. It would thus be of interest to incorporate awareness of right and left at least on the child's own body as a feature in predictive batteries, and to investigate, if possible, the extent of this relationship to somatosensory and to verbal symbolic determinants.

---

6. Silver and Hagin (1960) believe that abnormal responses on Schilder's arm extension test reflect cortical dominance more reliably than does ambiguous handedness.

VISUAL PERCEPTION

Visual perception is not a unitary process. Piaget, as quoted by Elkind and Scott (1962), stated: "Perception is not an immediately fixed mechanism for registering stimuli, but a developing system which becomes increasingly adaptive with age."

As is true for other aspects of development, the organization of visual perception in young children moves from gross to differentiated, from diffuse and unstable to more complex and better integrated. Piaget and Inhelder (1958) found, for instance, that in copying a figure such as a circle within a triangle preschool children correctly perceived each form but missed the relationship between the two, probably because the perceptual analysis and synthesis involved are developmentally later acquisitions. Children's copies of the Bender Gestalten show striking advances between the ages of five and seven.

Another characteristic of young children's visual perception is their difficulty with orientation in space. Gibson *et al.* (1962) and Neisser (1968) say that rotations and reversals are very frequent in young children but decrease rapidly with age, a statement which has been fully confirmed by clinicians and teachers. At age five, spatial orientation is still labile; lability of visual perceptual experiences often persists in children who suffer from reading and spelling difficulties at older ages.

Three visual competences, according to Weintraub (1967–68), are essential to reading: visual efficiency, both structural and functional; visual discrimination—the ability to distinguish between shapes; and visual perception, which adds meaning to what is seen. Visual perception depends on the two lower-level competences.

It is unfortunate that in the literature the term *visual perception* is applied to activities involving both nonverbal and verbal visual competences. As pointed out by Kolers (1969), the latter, which require symbolic functioning, are processed in a different part of the brain.

The predictive potential of visual perceptual competences has been explored by way of both nonverbal and verbal visual tasks and by a combination of the two. Goins (1958) investigated kindergarten children's performance on fourteen nonverbal visual tests, using pictures and designs. Seven of them correlated significantly with first-grade reading scores obtained eight months later. Interestingly, Pattern Copying, which is a complex task, had a higher correlation with reading than all others combined. Buktenica (1968), who used two of Goins' tests and one of his own, stated that performance on these kinds of tests accounted for 28 percent of the variance in end-of-first-grade reading. He contends that, because such tests are not "contaminated" with beginning reading activities, they evaluate "reading potential."

The present authors, however, agree with Barrett (1965a), who, in an excellent presentation of the subject, concluded that the predictive usefulness of nonverbal tests is limited and depends largely on the complexity of the tasks. In his own exhaustive study of 632 children, Barrett (1965b) investigated a *combination* of nonverbal and verbal visual stimuli (that is, letters and words) for predicting reading achievement. He concluded that two *verbal* visual tests, naming of letters and numbers, were the best single predictors.

Many researchers use solely verbal perceptual stimuli—letters and words—for purposes of prediction. Letter recognition, according to Gibson *et al.* (1962), requires discrimination between sets of configurations, very similar except for some "critical" feature which differentiates one letter from another. It is probable that symbolic functioning also contributes to what seems to be a purely perceptual performance.

In two large-scale investigations Olson (1958) and Gavel (1958) demonstrated the superiority of letter naming, which requires a higher degree of verbal symbolic functioning, over letter matching, which demands primarily a visual perceptual response. In Weiner and Feldmann's study (1950), identification of small and capital letters was a heavy contributor to the predictive formula, for which some correlations reached .90.

That verbal visual tasks are better predictors than nonverbal ones might be expected, because the closer in content a predictor variable is to a criterion measure, the closer will be the correlation between the two. It stands to reason that a child who is able to name letters before he is exposed to reading instruction will tend to do well in the early grades. However, we do not know whether the association between letter naming and subsequent reading achievement is a *causal* one. Does ability to name letters at an early age help children to read more effectively two or three years later? Or does early curiosity about letters prior to formal instruction reflect a quality in the child himself or in his environment which enables him to benefit optimally from stimulation? Durkin (1961) says early readers are children who *want* to read, who are consistently curious as to the meaning of printed signs. Sutton (1964) calls them "book hungry." Such behavior is, of course, encouraged in middle class homes. On the other hand, many intelligent five- and six-year-olds do not benefit from exposure to letters because they have not attained the developmental level that would enable them to benefit. And there are untold numbers of deprived children who have never been stimulated in this respect at all. At any rate the variable of home training prior to first-grade entrance has to be accounted for in prediction.

Visual perception plays a part during the early stages of reading but becomes far less important at higher grades when cognitive and, above all, linguistic competences move more and more into the foreground. In the final analysis, visual perception does not contribute enough to bear the entire burden of prediction (Barrett, 1965b).

BODY IMAGE AND VISUOMOTOR INTEGRATION

A child's body image, as reflected in his human-figure drawing, results from the integration of his proprioceptive, sensorimotor, emotional, and interpersonal experiences. Ability to
cope with spatial relationships (and printed words are patterns
laid out in space) originally derives from the child's awareness
of his own body, its parts, and the relationship of these parts to
one another. Thus, children's human-figure drawings might be
expected to have some predictive association with later reading
competence.

Coleman, Iscoe, and Brodsky (1959), and Shipps and Loudon
(1964), using Goodenough's scoring criteria, found a correlation
of .41 and .51 respectively between the Draw-A-Man Test
(1926) administered at the beginning of first grade and the
Metropolitan Achievement Test in the second grade. De Hirsch
and Jansky (1966) scored kindergarten children's human-figure
drawings in terms of their cohesiveness and differentiation,
thereby attempting to get some measure of integrative functioning. They found a weak but statistically significant correlation with reading and spelling achievement at the end of the
second grade.

There is a real question concerning the scoring of the Draw-
A-Man Test, which was originally devised by Goodenough as a
relatively culture-free nonverbal intelligence measure. If her
scoring is used, the predictive association between the test and
subsequent reading achievement may simply reflect, on a nonverbal level, the association between MA and later reading
achievement.

The Bender Motor Gestalt Test (1938), another instrument
for evaluating integrative competence and spatial organization,
has been used successfully for prediction. Koppitz *et al.* (1961)
administered the test to 272 beginning first-graders and found
a correlation of .68 with the Metropolitan Achievement Test at

the end of the year. In the study by de Hirsch, Jansky, *et al.* (1966) the Bender Gestalt proved to be one of the best predictors for reading performance thirty months later. An important paper by Bender (1967) discusses principles of scoring which apply also to the predictive use of the test.

The Draw-A-Man Test and the Bender Motor Gestalt Test probably do not measure single variables but clusters. Their main usefulness lies in their potential to evaluate integrative functions which are of considerable interest for prediction. These tests will, however, measure such functions only if scoring emphasizes the total configuration rather than details.

AUDITORY PERCEPTION

The importance of auditory perception for reading was recognized in the early thirties but was largely neglected during the next two decades. With the resurgence of interest in phonics, auditory perception is again being investigated in terms of prediction.

Among the various auditory perceptual skills, three dimensions—tracking and auditory sequencing, auditory memory span, and auditory discrimination—seem to be crucial for the reading task. It can be assumed that the three are interrelated.[7]

Stamback's early work (1951) points to the role of auditory sequencing even on a nonverbal level. She found that ability to imitate a series of tapped-out patterns was related to reading competence.

The sequencing of words in English constitutes an important linguistic signal. Reading requires "informed guessing" as to the probable direction of printed sequences. Thus, a positive relationship between auditory sequencing and reading could be

7. The interrelationship was shown for seven-year-olds by Jansky, who found that various aspects of auditory perception contributed to the same factor (Ph.D. thesis, 1970).

expected. In fact, clinicians find that children who scramble the order of sounds in words and of words in sentences—a phenomenon which reflects an input disorder—also have trouble with printed words.

The sequencing of auditory events[8] is closely related to auditory memory span, which, according to Masland and Case (1965), refers not only to the duration of attention but also to the number of bits of information which can be stored and recalled within a given time span. Auditory memory span is usually tested by repetition of numerical and verbal material: numbers, nonsense syllables, words, sentences. Repetition of sentences, however, probably depends not only on short-term memory but also on the length and complexity of units and, in turn, on the child's comprehension and use of syntactical structures (Menyuk, 1964). Further, Labov *et al.* (1968) report that, in repeating a sentence heard, ghetto children convert what they hear into their own language code. It is thus evident that the norms for auditory memory standardized on middle class children are not applicable to youngsters who speak a dialect.

Inferior auditory discrimination has been implicated in reading failure. In his review of previous studies Dykstra (1966) reported positive correlations ranging from .30 to .40. All seven of the auditory discrimination measures he administered to 632 children from three socioeconomic levels were related to later reading scores. It is of note that at kindergarten age, girls not only were significantly superior to boys on three auditory discrimination tasks but also were significantly better readers.

Dialect differences inevitably interfere with children's ability to discriminate between sounds of standard English. Gottesman (1968) and Baratz and Shuy (1969) point to the enormous difficulties of auditory discrimination tasks for children whose phonological system differs from that of the language used by teachers.

8. See Berry's excellent discussion (1969) of auditory perception.

We know that auditory discrimination and intelligence are related. We know, furthermore (Birch and Belmont, 1965b), that socioeconomic differences play a part. However, we know little about the nature of the interaction between social class, intelligence, and auditory discrimination. Are there underlying integrative functions which would explain these associations? It is of interest in this context that Blank (1968) believes that the association between auditory discrimination and reading reflects not auditory perceptual functions per se but a multiplicity of determinants including the ability to comply with cognitive demands such as listening to a sequence, retention of sequences in order to compare one stimulus with another, and judgment of similarities and differences. (The present authors have found that some young children's poor performance on auditory discrimination tests rests on their inability to manipulate verbal concepts as abstract as are "same" and "different.")

Related but different aspects of auditory perception, such as the sounding out of letters and ability to blend, have been considered in terms of prediction. Chall, Roswell, and Blumenthal (1963) found a substantial relationship between auditory blending in Grade I and reading competence in Grade III. It would be interesting to explore the contribution of generalized integrative competence to this relationship. On tasks involving auditory synthesis, moreover, variables such as short-term memory, attention, and impulsivity should be carefully checked.

Beyond these dimensions, there are other subtle but important aspects of auditory behavior which have been neglected in terms of prediction; trouble with processing of oral language, for instance, is a frequent source of difficulty with reading comprehension. The larger question then arises in how far the single separate aspects of auditory perception fuse in the service of the reading task.

In summary, it would be essential to investigate the complex interrelationships among the several aspects of auditory perception, intelligence, and socioeconomic status, including dialect differences, in terms of their predictive significance.

ORAL LANGUAGE

The literature, starting with Orton (1937), is replete with references to the close relationship between receptive and expressive aspects of oral language, on the one hand, and reading, on the other.[9]

Long before children enter school, they have mastered the basic phonological and grammatical rules of their language and function effectively on a verbal symbolic level. Young children bring their knowledge of linguistic structures to bear on the sentences they read and they expect them to conform to the oral-language structures with which they are familiar (Weber, 1968).

In an experimental study, Robinson (1963) found correlations of about .80 among vocabulary, reading, writing, listening, and speaking. Knowledge of word meanings and understanding of sentence structure are essential for reading comprehension.

Two interesting studies deal with the predictive potential of oral language *reception*. Moe (1957) reported that a single measure of "auding" ability derived from the children's interpretations of stories forecast reading performance as well as or better than either of two reading readiness tests or any of the psychometric measures used as alternative predictors.

Sister Marie Lauderville (1958) also found that a test of listening skills is as effective a predictor of later reading competence

9. Family history of reading problems, which according to Orton (1937) are related to a generalized language disability, has not been included here as a predictor variable. Although the senior author believes that there is a significant relationship between familial weakness in the language area and reading failure, there are few if any statistical *predictive* investigations involving this aspect. Nevertheless, attention is drawn to publications by Orton (1930), Eustis (1947), Hallgren (1950), and Hermann and Norrie (1958), all of whom have stressed genetic factors.

as are standardized reading readiness tests. She evaluated beginning first-graders on their ability to follow directions, note details, understand sequences, resolve main ideas, and make inferences.

In the *expressive*-language area, Clyde Martin (1955) found a negligible association between quantitative aspects of oral language (number of words, number of different words, and average length of sentences) and end-of-year reading scores. Quantitative dimensions may be less adequate measures of oral language than are aspects such as syntactic complexity.

Bougere (1969) demonstrated that the predictive power of the Metropolitan Reading Readiness Tests was improved by the addition of linguistic items—richness of vocabulary and complexity of syntactic forms, for example. Investigations centering prediction on ability to understand and generate grammatical structures are relatively recent. Developmental linguists, however, paved the way (Cazden, 1968; Brown and Bellugi, 1964; McNeill, 1970). As pointed out by Menyuk (1964), comprehension and use of forms, such as tenses, negations, questions, or embedding, are largely developmentally determined. The structure "he has been running," for instance, is used by only 14 percent of kindergarten children but by 41 percent of first-graders. Berko's (1958) ingenious tasks, which evaluate children's ability to use transformations, provide important information about their linguistic level. Lee's Northwestern Syntax Screening Test (1969), which assesses preschool children's linguistic maturity, may prove to be an interesting predictive tool.

Linguistic measures that have been standardized on middle class children, however, are not appropriate for youngsters from different social groups, whose phonemic and syntactic systems differ from standard English forms.

During the last decade a good deal of attention has been directed toward the association between deprived children's oral-language deficits (a concept which needs careful definition) and their failure in reading. The fact is, very little is known about whether the all-important shift from an action-oriented to a verbally oriented world, if it occurs at all, occurs at the same time among ghetto as among middle class children. Experimental studies are sorely needed to ascertain the timing of such shifts, because they are crucial for prediction.

INTERSENSORY INTEGRATION

In an early study Stamback (1951) suggested that children suffering from reading disabilities have great difficulty matching rhythmic taps against visual reproductions of patterns. Like reading, this task requires the translation of a sequence in space into a sequence in time.

Birch and Belmont (1965a) demonstrated that retarded readers have trouble converting temporally presented sequences of sounds into spatially presented series of visual patterns. They assume that such children have difficulty making judgments of auditory-visual equivalence. Muehl and Kremenack (1966), following the footsteps of Birch and Belmont, confirmed their findings. The authors stressed the need for early identification of deficits in the integration of information conveyed through auditory and visual pathways.

Blank and Bridger (1967), on the other hand, believe that what looks like a simple perceptual transaction, the making of equivalents between auditory and visual stimuli, actually requires a high level of conceptualization. They regard so-called cross-modal deficits as failure to code accurately the temporally presented components of the task.

Bryant (1968) and Johnson (1971) agree that actually we are dealing with *intra*modal difficulties. Further research is needed to explore the significance for prediction of intramodal difficulties and their relation to intersensory integration.

EMOTIONAL FACTORS

Most researchers argue that in children who present reading problems emotional difficulties may be the *result* rather than the cause of their academic failure. It should be pointed out, however, that a reading disorder does not preclude psychodynamic problems and that the two may exist concomitantly, reinforcing each other. Furthermore, children with subtle physiological deficits—and many youngsters with reading difficulties belong in this category—tend to be vulnerable to stress and anxiety prone. To tease apart the complex interactions between physiological, environmental, and psychological aspects of reading failure is no easy task. In many cases it is difficult to ascertain what, specifically, are the interactions between social and individual pathology. Muir *et al.* (1969) suggest that environmental stress may result in damage to essential ego functions which, in turn, interferes with learning.

In order to function in the elementary grades, the child must be ready to separate from home, he must be relatively free from conflicts belonging to developmentally earlier phases, and he must, at least up to a point, have learned to postpone gratification and to curb impulsivity. Impulsivity, as conceptualized by Kagan (1969), is the tendency to produce precipitous as opposed to reflective solutions. This kind of response seems to be more prevalent in lower than in middle class children. Clinicians and teachers know only too well that the inability to inhibit response seriously interferes with learning.

The following discussion is limited to a few studies concerned with the prediction of subsequent performance on the basis of an evaluation of emotional status at preschool age.

Lindemann *et al.* (1963) based their prognosis on ratings of the social and emotional adjustment of 174 children about to enter kindergarten, using doll play, interviews, and a history taken from the mother. Ratings were successful in predicting *superior* academic and emotional adjustment at end of first grade but failed to identify those children at the other extreme, the school failures.

Wattenberg and Clifford (1964) explored the relationship of beginning reading achievement with self-concept and ego strength at the kindergarten level. Ten of 28 measures of self-concept were significantly related to later performance; a similar association was found for ego strength. In the study by de Hirsch, Jansky, *et al.* (1966), ego strength, assessed clinically, was also found to be significantly associated with reading and spelling scores thirty months later.

Meyer (1953) examined the potential of the Rorschach Test administered at kindergarten age for predicting achievement at the beginning of third grade. The results indicated that inaccurate, vague, and mediocre global perception, as well as poor rapport with the environment, distinguished failing readers from those who passed. Ames and Walker (1964), testing Meyer's findings, administered the Rorschach and the WISC to kindergarten children whose reading achievement was subsequently evaluated at fifth grade. The correlation between the prognostic index and reading level was .53. "The greater use of color and movement by the better reader groups . . . evidently reflected their greater emotional maturity, more differentiated experience and greater openness to stimulation."

Muir *et al.* (1969), who attempted to evaluate the relationship between Piaget's developmental categories and a Neuroticism Scale constructed for the purpose, found that increased neuroticism was associated with decreasing cognitive skills. While the Neuroticism Scale may need revision, the study is of considerable interest because it appears to show what Piaget calls the indivisibility of cognitive and affective functioning.

In the framework of psychoanalytically oriented psychology, earlier researchers—Blanchard (1946) and Sperry *et al.* (1958), for example—drew attention to the association between reading difficulties and categories such as parental pathology, and in the case of children, inhibition of curiosity or withdrawal from competition.

During the last decade ego disturbances have been the focus of attention in cases of learning failure. Unfortunately, there has been no attempt to use Anna Freud's Developmental Lines (1965) to predict school achievement. She considers ability to control, inhibit, and modify impulses and to use them constructively in the service of a long-term goal a sine qua non for learning. In order to succeed in school, according to Anna Freud, "the child must carry out preconceived plans with a minimum regard for the lack of immediate pleasure yield, intervening frustration and maximum regard for the ultimate outcome." In other words, he must have made the transition from the pleasure to the reality principle. Investigations along these lines are long overdue. To raise only two of many questions: Can one predict subsequent reading achievement on the basis of the preschool child's ability to control impulses and postpone gratification? Does an unusual degree of passivity and dependency at age four and five point to later failures?

Projective testing together with a clinical examination of the child might enable investigators to explore such variables for prediction.

Prediction from Combination of Variables

The child entering school brings to this new situation the quality of affect that has nourished him in the past, the environment in which he has grown up, his social, cultural, and economic background, and his cognitive endowment. The trend among researchers toward a more complex approach to the problems of prediction is reflected in a tendency to devise batteries that forecast from a broader basis. Most investigators agree that a combination of variables yields a higher level of predictive accuracy than any isolated variable.

READING READINESS TESTS

Austin and Morrison (1963) reported that more than 80 percent of the schools contacted nationally used reading readiness tests before exposing children to formal reading instruction. The professed aims of these tests are: (1) to identify pupils likely to fail in the primary grades and (2) to pinpoint individual children's deficits in skills believed to be implicated in reading failure.

Among the best known of the many widely used reading readiness tests are the Gates-MacGinitie Reading Readiness Test (1968), the Metropolitan Readiness Test (Hildreth and Griffiths, 1950), and the Lee-Clark Reading Readiness Test, 1962 Revision, which will not need to be described here because educators are well acquainted with them.[10] The Gates-MacGinitie provides norms against which a given child's performance can be compared; the other two present expectancy tables in which scores are categorized according to readiness levels.

A large number of reading readiness tests use multiple correlation and regression analysis to examine the relation between readiness scores and subsequent achievement. The coefficients of correlation found in these instruments, which use different samples and different achievement criteria, are quite constant and range from .40 to .60, with a few extremes at either end; they demonstrate the moderate predictive usefulness of these tests (Dykstra, 1967). It should be added that some investigators (Karlin, 1957; Weintraub, 1967) maintain that these instruments do an adequate job only at the extremes of the normal curve. Others (Bagford, 1968; Kingston, 1962) say that their

10. A recent report by Johnson (1969) suggests that the Clymer-Barrett Prereading Battery predicts success more accurately than does the Metropolitan Readiness Test.

usefulness extends into the third and fourth grade. There is uniform agreement that the tests do not predict accurately for individual children.

In this context, Dykstra (1967) raised the issue of the *practical* significance for the teacher of a correlation coefficient in the range from .50 to .60. The teacher expects that pupils who score well on reading readiness tests will be the best readers and that those who do poorly will achieve at a low level. In a study directed to this issue Fendric and McGlade (1938) found that pupils who have high scores on readiness tests do, in fact, learn to read well. Predictions are far less valid for children who score poorly. Bremer (1959), who classified pupils as low, average, or high on the basis of their performance on the Metropolitan Readiness Test, found that one-third of the low-readiness group scored above average on reading at the end of the first grade. Spache (1965) developed expectancy tables for each of four experimental groups to predict end-of-first-grade reading achievement and concluded: "These tables afford the teacher little assistance on the basis of September performance."

Dykstra discussed another important problem: To what extent do readiness tests measure the skills they set out to measure? In his own investigation, cited earlier, the intercorrelations between several auditory measures were so low that it was doubtful whether they evaluated the same dimensions. There is the possibility, of course, that either the tests were not reliable or auditory discrimination is not a unitary competence. A child might fail this task because it is too abstract, because he is unable to mobilize energy in the service of a goal that makes little sense to him, or because impulsivity prevents him from functioning. Before deciding whether the child has genuine difficulties with auditory discrimination, which is what the task purports to evaluate, one must determine what, in fact, is being measured. From an instructional point of view it is not sufficient to know that a test correlates highly with subsequent achievement. Appropriate intervention can be initiated only if the competence on which the tests are based is clearly identified. Dykstra (1968) therefore, expressed the urgent need for factor analysis to determine the competences subsumed under a large variety of predictive tests.

Reading readiness tests consist of a number of subtests which presumably measure different competences. To investigate this hypothesis, Lowell (1967) performed a factor analysis of the Lee-Clark, the Murphy-Durrell, and Tests of General Ability (TOGA). He found that the tests in the Murphy-Durrell reflected only a single underlying ability. Analysis of the Lee-Clark and the TOGA tests uncovered two factors, one for boys and one for girls. This finding suggests that many readiness instruments may assess only a single aspect of prediction. Lowell concluded that they are not as good predictors as is desirable, but that predictive efficacy could be improved if a composite of subtests from different batteries were used.

In an effort to evaluate the usefulness of individual *subtests,* the Cooperative Research Program in First Grade Reading Instruction (Bond and Dykstra, 1967) found the Murphy-Durrell Letter Naming Test to be the best single predictor. The results of a multiple regression analysis of a variety of prereading dimensions, such as auditory and visual discrimination, mental age, socioeconomic status, and so forth, suggested to Silvaroli (1965) that "the single factor of letter identification can be used to predict reading achievement as well as or better than any other combination of the readiness factors used in the present study." The fact is that no single subtest provides anything like adequate information about an individual child's weakness and strength. Moreover, ability to name letters depends heavily on exposure.[11] In a study of Home Reading Experiences and first-grade reading achievement, Miller (1967) found a relationship between social class and knowledge of letter names.

11. How far *Sesame Street* has modified predictive correlations for this particular test has not yet been assessed.

Finally, are reading readiness instruments better predictors than certain other measures? Dykstra (1967) concluded that ratings on intelligence tests, number concepts, Bender Gestalt, Rorschach, and, above all, teachers' judgments predict performance as well as do conventional readiness tests.

A word should be added here concerning administration. If the goal of reading readiness tests is to present a diagnostic profile of individual children, group administration is not a suitable procedure. From the mere score on the Word Matching Section of the Gates Reading Readiness Test, for instance, it is impossible to know *why* a child has failed. He may not have understood the directions, which assume familiarity with concepts such as "same" and "different." He may have found the many printed signs on the page too confusing because of figure-ground problems. He may have lacked the organizational ability to handle the rather complex task, or he may have been unable to sustain attention. Or, finally, he may have inferior perceptual ability, which is what the test purports to evaluate. In other words, his percentile score alone would be of little help in devising interventional strategies—which is the ultimate purpose of prediction.

PREDICTIVE TEST BATTERIES

Up to a point, the choice of tests included in a predictive battery reflects the researcher's theoretical bias as to what constitutes the reading process. In the following pages are listed some of the more representative clinical and statistical batteries.

The outstanding early instrument was Monroe's (1935), which included a wide variety of tasks. After some years of neglect it is now being used again in a number of schools. The expectancy tables prepared by Monroe indicated that the percentage range between 40 percent and 60 percent was the least stable. Above this range performance was so good, and below it, so poor, that extraneous factors were of relatively little importance. It was around the median that psychological and teaching determinants made the difference between success and failure. Monroe emphasized that reading disability is due, not to any single defect, but rather to a combination of deficits and that tests—predictive or not—can never replace a careful diagnosis of a child's difficulties.

Jean Simon (1952) administered a battery of tests, most of them heavily weighted in the direction of cognitive functioning, at the end of pupils' kindergarten year. He provided a cutoff point below which failure in reading was believed to be probable. Predictions made on this basis were correct about 85 percent of the time. He concluded that inability to abstract and analyze is the characteristic feature in reading failure.

The battery developed by Inizan (1966) included some tests from the Simon instrument, in addition to eight tests from a Brazilian battery. Interestingly, Inizan prepared expectancy tables in which chronological age and the child's scores on the predictive battery were combined to estimate how many months it would take him to learn to read.

Hirst (1969) followed a group of kindergarten children from three different socioeconomic levels through the second grade. With a two-year interval between prediction and outcome, her battery accounted for 37 percent of the variance in reading at the end of the second grade.

Feldmann and Hilton (personal communication, 1971) have developed a Pre-Reading Skills Battery based on the performance of middle and lower class kindergarten children from various ethnic backgrounds. The battery consists of thirteen paper-and-pencil, group-administered tests. Evaluation of skills in the areas of language and of visual and auditory perception provides a diagnostic picture of the child's prereading competences. The authors aim at a developmental approach through use of tests of the same skills at different levels of complexity.

As has been pointed out, most instruments express predictive relationships by correlation coefficients. The authors agree with Dykstra (1968) that a coefficient is little more than a rough indicator of predictive power. Predictive instruments should provide cutoff points separating eventually passing from failing readers.

TEACHERS' ASSESSMENTS

Kindergarten teachers' assessments of their pupils, distilled from a variety of observations in the classroom, are used by a fairly large number of schools in the prediction of later academic achievement. The fact that kindergarten teachers are more developmentally oriented than subject oriented is an asset, and their predictions are often remarkably accurate.

In a summary of a number of studies dealing with the relationship between kindergarten teachers' ratings and subsequent reading performance, Bliesmer (1951) found correlation coefficients ranging from .50 to .80, with one or two reporting correlations over .85. These coefficients are higher than those for other potential predictors. The excellence of teachers' predictions has been confirmed by many recent studies.

It is of interest to speculate why teachers' evaluations of later functioning are so effective. There is, of course, the fact that teachers have unique opportunities to observe their pupils in a variety of situations and over an extended period of time. They know how strongly individual children are motivated; they know their frustration threshold and their ability to work for a distant goal. Teachers, like clinicians, rely heavily on both intuition and experience. This makes their judgment more rather than less valuable, even if not all teachers are able to verbalize the bases for their assessments. A teacher might say: "This boy holds the pencil as awkwardly as the one who sits next to him, and he has the same trouble attaching names to letter shapes, but *he* will make the grade and the other boy won't." If an attempt is made to find out what it is that, in the teacher's eyes, distinguishes the one who "will make it" from the one who will not, the result is usually a description such as "enthusiastic" or some other not easily definable attribute which *does* make the difference.

Such assessments depend of course in large degree on the individual teacher's sensitivity, know-how, and familiarity with the particular ethnic group in question.[12] Ability to predict differs markedly from teacher to teacher, and assessments cannot readily be duplicated.

The gifted teacher's apperception of the child's total functioning, which is not the same as the sum of his strengths and deficits, is the very quality that makes it hard to duplicate these evaluations and is probably the very one that makes them useful. Until statistical procedures are available which make it possible to ascertain the relative contribution of specific deficits to the overall picture, and above all until we know more about the process of compensation, teachers' assessments will continue to rank high among predictors.

Theoretical Considerations

In reviewing past studies one misses an exploration of at least three basic issues:

One involves the question of what exactly is being predicted and for whom. Do we need different instruments to predict for different reading levels? And do we need different instruments for different subgroups of readers?

12. In Hirst's study (1969), kindergarten teachers' predictions were highly significant for the lower socioeconomic group. Low expectations, Hirst says, might result in low achievement. The question has been raised (Rosenthal and Jacobson, 1968) whether in some cases the principle of "self-fulfilling prophecy" is operating. Thorndike (1968) has attacked this exposition, mainly because of the inadequacy of the conclusions drawn from the data.

The second focuses upon the problem of quantification. To what extent does quantification lead to neglect of parameters important for prediction?

The third is related to the complex interactions among single predictive variables.

A predictive model "utilizes a set of initial findings to anticipate the nature of an eventual state" (Thomas *et al.*, 1963). Underlying the concept of prediction are two assumptions: that development is by and large a consistent process and that individuals for whom predictions are made will continue in "expected environments."

In the case of reading prediction it is essential to specify what is meant by the "eventual state." What is actually being predicted? Wiener and Cromer's model (1967) allows for multiple antecedents and for multiple consequents.

Since success in reading is related to different determinants at different stages of the reading task, it is imperative to clarify whether a given instrument predicts for early reading—that is, decoding[13] and word identification and analysis—or mature reading. Early reading is primarily concerned with skills which may be necessary antecedents of mature reading. Some of them, such as vocalizing during silent reading, drop out when the process becomes automatic but may still be observed when the reader is confronted with a difficult passage.

Mature reading assumes the mastery of subskills and implies the comprehension of syntactical relationships, the derivation of meaning, and the construction of anticipatory schemata. It requires, furthermore, the assimilation of content into an already existing contextual framework. In the accomplished reader there is a direct road from printed input to meaning (Kainz, 1956). In a fascinating study Smith and Holmes (1971)

13. Goodman (1965) rightly points out that the word *decoding* is misleading. In information theory, *decoding* means going from code to message. Translating from graphic input to speech, which is then decoded for meaning, as it is in listening, might better be described as *recoding*.

assert that skilled readers do not identify letters en route to words, nor is there any evidence that in reading for comprehension fluent readers identify single words. These authors maintain, as do Goodman (1965) and Kolers (1969), that reading is not primarily visual, that for the fluent reader much of the visual information is highly redundant.[14]

The nature of the reading task changes as children move from lower into higher grades. As interpretation of complex syntactical structures, involvement in subject matter, and capacity to make inferences move into the foreground, perceptual factors recede in the background and diminish in importance (Bryan, 1964).

The first issue, then, is the definition of predictive goals, the level of reading for which an instrument predicts (Clymer, 1969). This definition determines criterion measures. Word-recognition tests may possibly suffice as criteria for the earliest skills; oral and silent reading comprehension tests are a minimum requirement at more advanced levels.

However, the fact that the reading differs for various subgroups complicates prediction. The middle class child decodes printed signs into his own language. The youngster who speaks a dialect must translate what he reads into a code that differs from the one on the printed page.

Differing criterion measures, therefore, may be required for various subgroups of children. Clearly, oral reading tests which require standard English responses are not suitable for pupils whose phonemic and grammatical systems differ. Although such children might fully comprehend what they read, they will tend to use their own linguistic forms when reading aloud, and hence, they may be penalized unjustly for errors on oral reading tests.

14. While it is true that beginning readers need more visual clues than do skilled readers, the author agrees with Ryan and Semmel (1969) that this distinction is useful only up to a point and that beginning reading involves many of the strategies used in advanced reading.

The following questions therefore arise: (1) Do we need differentially constructed instruments to predict early as against mature reading? (2) Do we need different instruments for children who speak nonstandard dialects, and for those from foreign-language backgrounds? In order to draw valid generalizations for such groups, we will need to study them separately, using the largest number of children and the most varied types of measurements possible.

The problem of quantification is a thorny one. Nobody questions the necessity of quantification in the case of epidemiological studies. But Escalona and Heider (1959) say that psychological research suffers not only from a lack of quantitative rigor; certain types of data preclude tests of significance. As pointed out by Dykstra (1968), certain dimensions which might be fruitful for prediction are not explored because they are difficult to quantify. When the senior author asked a researcher who investigated the characteristics of mothers of young children how many of them were able to enjoy their babies, he answered that he had not pursued this topic because it was too difficult to quantify.

It is often said that present limitations of quantitative approaches will be resolved by the use of more refined techniques. Improved techniques will not, however, take care of the problem because quantification tends to change in subtle or not so subtle ways the very nature of the questions posed. Moreover, findings resulting from quantified research often lack the subtlety and sophistication which are hallmarks of first-class clinical endeavors. Gordon (1970) comments that educational research has been dominated by hypothesis testing or verification to the neglect of investigations based on careful and systematic observations.

Attention is a case in point. Gibson (1963) says that although this concept has been attacked as too vague, nobody questions its meaning. It is a powerful selector of input; it allows for "focal points in stimulus arrays, and it serves to exclude non-pertinent stimuli." The ability to focus attention, however, is closely related to affective factors, and one can hardly discuss attention without taking into account motivation. Motivation, Schwartz and Schiller (1970) suggest, polarizes the field and determines what is relevant. Clinical studies might be better suited to explore attention and its relation to motivation than quantitative ones. Such studies might show that this variable contributes heavily to prediction.

Psychodynamic dimensions have never received sufficient consideration, largely because they present specific difficulties in terms of quantification. One example might suffice: Anxiety at early ages is assumed to augur poor reading in later years. In some cases, however, anxiety may be a spur to learning. What has to be assessed is the degree and kind of anxiety that immobilizes the learner, and this type of subtle assessment is extremely difficult to achieve by quantitative measures. It is more or less accepted that characteristics such as ego strength may make the difference between success and failure. A child may have trouble matching letters and word shapes at preschool level, but if he has a healthy curiosity,[15] if he is excited about learning, he may do better than a passive youngster who does not have his heart in his work and who does not push through. Ego strength, like other psychological dimensions, is hard to quantify.

Quality of teaching, which Bond and Dykstra (1967) found to be far more important than methods used in instruction, is another parameter which is not easy to assess quantitatively (Harris, 1969). Nevertheless, it is common knowledge that the teacher's training and competence, her commitment to the task, her flexibility, and her empathy with children from various subcultures are important determinants in the educational pro-

15. Minuchin (1971) developed measures of curiosity and exploration in preschool children. Her data describe a "developmental high risk" group in terms of these dimensions, particularly among disadvantaged youngsters.

cess. It would be desirable, moreover, to arrive at some formulation as to what type of teacher would best fit with certain groups. Some are more successful when they teach early skills; others do better at advanced levels. Many teachers are far more comfortable with middle class than with deprived pupils. While supervisors' ratings of teachers' effectiveness are known to be poor (Bond and Dykstra, 1967), experienced teachers' observations as to the qualities which make for success might form the basis for rating scales such as Ryans' (1960).[16] These scales might be tried out in terms of their predictive usefulness.

Another dimension which has been neglected is the value system young children bring to school. The values of nonwhite preschool youngsters of working class parents differ in significant ways from those of their middle class peers (Hertzig *et al.*, 1968). In an interesting paper, Ermalinski and Ruscelli (1971) compared middle and lower class boys in a day care center on behaviors such as cleanliness, honesty, and cooperation, all much appreciated by middle class teachers. They found that the lower class children obtained lower scores on cleanliness and honesty. While these aspects might lend themselves to quantification, it would be difficult to quantify the teachers' responses to such characteristics. The teacher might not know consciously that she has difficulty accepting these children, but her unconscious negative feelings might well affect her pupils' performance and thus indirectly influence prediction. Problems centering around value systems raise a host of sensitive questions and deserve careful and, if possible, unbiased investigation.

Predictive batteries, thus, should not be limited to tests which measure directly observable behavior. Subjective data have their place. Defined operationally, and assessed by observations

16. St. John (1971) used a modification of Ryans' scales to rate teachers. She found that length of teacher service was not related to reading gains in black children. Child-focused teachers were more successful than the curriculum-oriented.

of experienced judges, such data can be translated into rating scales. Integration of these data into predictive batteries might yield richer and more differentiated predictive profiles.

Indeed, there is no reason why predictive studies should all be of a statistical variety. The field of prediction might benefit from longitudinal studies of individual children. Such studies might teach us a good deal about the interaction among genetic, neurophysiological, cultural, and psychological determinants, and might result in more subtle hypotheses, which could then form the basis of statistical investigations.

The problem of interaction among predictive variables is a crucial issue. Birch (1970) believes that interactive effects may be far more important than those stemming from the variables themselves. These effects will vary according to each child's cognitive endowment; his adaptive capacity, including his vulnerability to stress; and the environmental forces impinging upon him (Lambert, 1967). Clinical judgment in any field is reached by the careful weighing of separate pieces of evidence and the often subtle and complex interactions among them, resulting in an appraisal of the total configuration. Unfortunately, this is not always what happens in educational diagnosis. The temptation to look at so complex a phenomenon as reading in a simplistic way is evidently considerable. Prognostic investigations should not result in a collection of single items. We need to search for sophisticated procedures which allow for assessments as differentiated as the best clinical evaluations.

Thus we come directly to the central importance of compensation as it relates to learning. Many children compensate for even massive deficits by using competences in other areas of functioning. For example, although visuomotor competence correlates highly with later reading performance, there are those who excel in spite of glaring visuomotor deficiencies. We do not know enough about the specific mechanism of compensation, nor do we know why some children fail to compensate. Psychological maturity, ego strength, intelligence, and a favorable environment undoubtedly play a part. It is well known that slum children compensate less effectively for organic deficits than do others, perhaps because less nurture is available to them physiologically and psychologically. Failure to take the variable of compensation into account as it interacts with the child's pattern of deficits and strengths will be reflected in uncertain predictions.

The instruments described in Chapters 2 and 3 represent an attempt to translate these theoretical considerations into a practical attack on prediction and diagnosis. These instruments are adapted to the characteristics of various subgroups; factor analysis was used to define the abilities underlying individual tests; and procedures were devised for integrating subjective data with objective information in order to arrive at a rounded picture of the child's functioning.

CHAPTER 2

A New Plan for Prediction

JEANNETTE JANSKY

The central concern of this book is a comprehensive plan for identification and diagnosis of children at risk of failing in reading. This plan reflects some of the theoretical positions outlined in the preceding chapter and is practical for individual administration in large groups.

Separate instruments were developed for predictive screening and for diagnosis. The rationales for the two differ. The aim of screening is pragmatic: to identify as many as possible of those children who are going to fail in the elementary grades. The aim of diagnosis is to develop profiles of individual children's weaknesses and strengths, thus pointing the way to timely and highly specific intervention.

The screening battery is designed to be administered in the spring of the kindergarten year. Performance on the tests should forecast a child's reading level after two years of schooling. The procedures described are appropriate for screening large populations. They are easy to teach to school personnel and paraprofessionals and are applicable for children from diverse social backgrounds with IQs ranging from high to low.

This battery was constructed with full awareness of the pitfalls of prediction. Development is, by and large, a consistent process, but at the critical ages between five and seven, children mature by fits and starts, alternating between regressive and forward movement. Such maturational irregularities are bound to interfere with prediction. Intervening variables like severe illness, upheavals in the child's family background, and frequent change of schools render predictions hazardous; differences in the teachers' competence might also influence outcome.

Nevertheless, even at early ages and despite maturational variability and the effects of external events, children show highly individualistic styles of responding, patterns of weakness and strength that constitute themes extending through successive phases of development. These themes reflect the stamp or characteristic quality of the individual learner.

Because of the inherent complexities of the maturational process and the vicissitudes of children's lives, prediction requires more than manipulation of test scores. It calls for flexible sifting and weighing of data concerning many aspects of the child's functioning within the framework of the demands of a given academic setting. Information obtained from a single source will not suffice. Evaluation can be reduced neither to the "hard" data of psychometricians nor to impressionistic judgments made by teachers. The problem necessitates the exploration of all possible avenues of information.

The predictive procedures described here demonstrate how to combine objective and subjective data. Integration of both kinds of material should result in far more differentiated predictive evaluations than are now in use.

Background of the Study

The research presented here was based on a pilot investigation (de Hirsch, Jansky, *et al.*, 1966). The goal of the early study was to identify at kindergarten level those children who were at risk of failing reading at the end of second grade. The subjects were fifty-three children to whom were administered thirty-seven tests in the areas of motility, gross and fine motor patterning, body image, laterality, visual and auditory perception, receptive and expressive language, and prereading. Estimates of behavioral style were added. Scores on these kindergarten tests were correlated with end-of-second-grade reading, spelling, and writing scores. Of the nineteen measures with statistically significant coefficients of correlation, the ten that best differentiated between failing and passing readers were finally selected to constitute a Predictive Index. This Index correctly identified ten of the eleven children who failed at the end of the second grade.

Most readiness tests simply determine where a child's score lies with respect to the normative group. The pilot study, in contrast, used kindergarten test findings to make projections as to each child's future status. Although this procedure has certain pitfalls, it is highly responsive to the needs of teachers and school systems.

The original Predictive Index had a number of important limitations. The extent to which the procedures could be generalized to new groups was restricted in several ways: Self-selection in the early study might have resulted in an atypical sample because only those children participated whose parents were willing to bring them for evaluation; the sample size was too small to permit development of criteria for various subgroups; the IQ range was restricted to 90 to 116; and the socioeconomic status of the group was more homogeneous than was desirable. From a methodological point of view, furthermore, the statistical procedures used in the pilot study did not allow differential weighting of predictive tests according to the extent of contribution to prediction. Moreover, administration of the ten-test battery was far too time-consuming. Finally, the test had to be given by highly trained and often overworked professionals.

The need for an epidemiological approach to prediction has become more urgent in recent years. Clearly, there is a demand for a short predictive instrument that can be administered by paraprofessionals and teachers. It was hoped that such a new instrument would incorporate the insights derived from the original research.[1]

Sample

Subjects for the present study were drawn from five public schools in two districts in New York City. The kindergarten tests were administered to all children who spoke and understood conversational English; this procedure yielded a total of 508 subjects. Of this group, only 341 continued to attend the schools in which they had originally been enrolled and were available when reading and spelling tests were administered two years later. Permission was obtained to test forty-nine pupils from the original group who had transferred to two parochial schools upon entering first grade; in addition, eleven public school children were evaluated at their new schools. Thus, the final sample size was 401.

The composition of the sample was inevitably determined by the ethnic and socioeconomic character of the neighborhoods served by the two school districts. Although the population of one district was predominantly black, it also included families of Puerto Rican, Italian, Irish, and Polish descent. The other district served largely Jewish and Italian families.

Table 1 shows sample characteristics in terms of sex, race, age, socioeconomic status, and intelligence (expressed in standard scores on the Similarities and Block Design subtests of the Wechsler Intelligence Scale for Children).

The sample included 217 boys and 184 girls. More than half the children were white, 42 percent were black, 5 percent were Puerto Rican, and three children were orientals. At the end of

1. The follow-up investigation of the original Predictive Index is fully described in Appendix A.

Table 1. Sample Characteristics

Race and Sex	Kindergarten Age (in months) Range: 63–77			Intelligence (WISC Similar.) Range: 0–20			Intelligence (WISC Blocks) Range: 0–19			SES Index Range: 3–11		
	N	Mean	SD	N	Mean	SD	N	Mean	SD	N	Mean	SD
White												
Males	122	69.8	3.44	52	12.0	3.97	50	11.6	3.10	88	4.0	2.66
Females	86	69.4	3.73	37	12.9	2.99	35	11.6	2.64	68	4.5	2.59
Total White	208	69.6	3.57	89	12.4	3.63	85	11.6	2.92	156	4.4	2.63
Black												
Males	82	69.9	3.80	28	11.1	3.40	26	10.0	3.08	54	7.1	1.93
Females	88	69.8	3.65	33	11.4	3.09	32	8.7	2.28	60	6.6	2.10
Total Black	170	69.9	3.72	61	11.3	3.24	58	9.3	2.75	114	6.8	2.04
Puerto Rican												
Males	12	72.1	1.75	5	10.0	5.06	5	9.4	1.96	9	7.1	2.64
Females	8	70.8	3.07	5	11.0	2.45	5	10.0	1.41	6	7.0	1.00
Total P.R.	20	71.6	2.46	10	10.5	4.00	10	9.7	1.74	15	7.1	2.14
Chinese												
Males	1	66.0	—	0			0			0		
Females	2	66.5	2.50	1	13.0	—	1	11.0	—	0		
Total Ch.	3	66.3	2.06	1	13.0	—	1	11.0	—	0		
Total	401	69.7	3.61	161	11.8	3.55	154	10.6	3.01	285	5.5	2.67

the kindergarten year the white and the black children were approximately 5 years, 10 months old, the Puerto Rican boys and girls were somewhat older, and the orientals were a little younger.

The socioeconomic rating system, based on parental occupation, educational attainment, and total family income, is presented in Appendix B. Such information could not be obtained for all pupils. Although an attempt was made to reach all parents, only about three-fourths of them were available and willing to provide these data. Average socioeconomic status for whites was nearly a standard deviation higher than that for blacks and Puerto Ricans.

Intelligence subtests, which were administered when the children were second-graders, were given only to a randomly selected subsample because there was not enough time to test all of the youngsters. The children as a group tended to receive higher-than-average scores on the measure of verbal intelligence (WISC Similarities). The greatest difference in subgroup means was between white girls and Puerto Rican boys. Black girls were the only children who fell below the average on the Performance Scale subtest (WISC Block Designs).

Sample size was reduced for the multiple correlation and regression analyses because the computer program for these procedures had no way to account for occasionally missing single test scores for individual children. Altogether, 347 children had complete sets of scores. Means for chronological age, intelligence, and socioeconomic status for black and for white boys and girls were substantially the same for this slightly smaller group as for the total sample.

Testing

The preschool tests were administered to the children at their schools in March, April, and May of their kindergarten year. Reading and spelling evaluation was undertaken in the spring of the second grade. In order to randomize the order of testing, the examiners drew subjects by identification number from a pool. With two exceptions, all tests were administered individually; the silent reading and spelling tests were administered to groups of three to five.

Nine examiners participated in the testing. Six of them were available for both the kindergarten and second-grade phases. Five were remedial reading teachers, three of whom had considerable testing experience. The other four were nonprofessionals. All examiners were carefully trained and supervised by the investigator. Training for kindergarten and second-grade administration involved two sessions each in which methodology was explained. In both phases each examiner pretested four nonstudy children and scored their kindergarten and second-grade protocols.

KINDERGARTEN TEST POOL

The predictive screening battery was drawn from a pool of tests which were considered potential predictors.

The choice of tests in the pool was based upon their prognostic usefulness in clinical practice, as well as on their predictive efficacy as established in our past research. The tests were selected primarily for their significance for the child's maturational status.

The following aspects of development were considered; perceptuomotor organization, linguistic competence in both its receptive and expressive aspects, and readiness to cope with printed symbols. The heavy emphasis on linguistic tests derived from the author's conviction that ability to comprehend and use oral language is of overwhelming importance in learning to read. It was hypothesized that a kindergarten child's standing in these competences would forecast his later performance in reading, writing, and spelling.

Thirteen of the kindergarten tests from the pilot study were used in the present project. Several additional tests were selected so as to increase the number of measures in certain categories. For example, some oral-language tests were added because of the feeling that originally there had been too few of them.

With great reluctance it was decided not to attempt to incorporate judgments of emotional maturity and ego strength. An important consideration was the lack of training of some of the examiners. At both kindergarten and second-grade levels, however, each examiner was directed to make an informal, behaviorally supported statement about the child's interest in the tests, his willingness to work, his ability to withstand frustration, and, to the extent the examiners were able to assess it, his anxiety level. After completion of all testing, two of the examiners used these observations to make effort ratings based on the child's vigor and persistence in approaching the kindergarten and second-grade tests.

Some of the tests were standardized; others were designed by the author.

The tests in the kindergarten pool are listed below. The ten that comprised the pilot study index are starred. These tests are fully described in the final two appendixes.

*1. Pencil Use
 2. Name Writing
*3. Bender Motor Gestalt Test
 4. Minnesota Percepto Diagnostic Test
 5. Tapped Patterns
 6. Sentence Memory (Forms L and M of the 1937 Stanford-Binet Intelligence Scale)
*7. Wepman Auditory Discrimination Test
 8. Boston Speech Sound Discrimination Test
 9. Roswell-Chall Auditory Blending Test
 10. Oral Language Level

*11. Number of Words Used in Telling a Story[2]
*12. Category Names
 13. Picture Naming
 14. Letter Naming
*15. Horst Nonsense Word Matching Test
*16. Word Matching Subtest of the 1937 Gates Reading Readiness Test
 17. Matching by Configuration (based on Gates)
*18. Recognition of Words Previously Taught ("boy" and "train")
*19. Spelling Two Words Previously Taught

The rationale for including the tests that were new to the present study may be summarized as follows:

Minnesota Percepto Diagnostic Test (Test 4). It was thought possible that the child's tendency to rotate nonverbal printed configurations might reflect some underlying difficulty with stabilization of verbal patterns set out in space; this, in turn, might be indicative of inability to manage printed verbal patterns distributed in space. The Minnesota test involved the copying of designs and was scored according to extent of rotation from the horizontal axis.

Sentence Memory (Forms L and M of the 1937 Stanford-Binet Intelligence Scale) (Test 6). Sentence memory is assumed to measure ability to store and to recall meaningful verbal sequences for short periods. In the author's opinion, sentence memory is also related to what might be called "sentence sense," or the ability to anticipate an unfamiliar word by virtue of clues provided by the surrounding syntactic configuration. Sentence memory might be a good predictor of reading because the ability to make correct guesses from the available

2. In the pilot research number of words was estimated by counting the words used in telling the story of "The Three Bears." For the present study, two cartoon series were chosen to elicit stories because in the early research children's familiarity with "The Three Bears" varied widely.

options is as essential for reading as for speech. The "guesses" of poor readers often reflect choices that are not acceptable linguistically or contextually.

Boston Speech Sound Discrimination Test (Test 8). For this task the child is asked to point to pairs of pictures named by the examiner. The use of pictures eliminates the necessity for spoken responses; it also facilitates the task for children who have trouble with concepts such as "same" and "different." It was recognized, on the other hand, that the introduction of visual stimuli might change the nature of the task.

Roswell-Chall Blending Test (Test 9). The Roswell-Chall test requires the subject to synthesize whole words from their parts as spoken by the examiner. It was believed that ability to form words from spoken segments would facilitate blending of printed words and thus reading.

Oral Language Level (Test 10). One would expect competence in reading to reflect the richness of the child's spoken-language resources. Therefore, the author tried to devise a single comprehensive measure of language maturity. The children were shown cartoon sequences and asked to tell stories about them. These stories were tape-recorded, and each child's spoken account was subsequently rated by two competent judges on the basis of maturity of articulatory patterning, sophistication of syntax, and cohesiveness of story organization.

Picture Naming (Test 13). The subjects were shown pictures of twenty-two objects and asked to name them. Over the years, the author has been strongly impressed by the struggle of most poor readers to evoke spoken equivalents of printed verbal referents. Children who present dysnomic features find it hard to recall whole words and letter names. It is often overlooked that they tend to forget phonic equivalents as well. At younger ages such dysnomic children have trouble learning color names, although they can match colors. At kindergarten level they forget the names of movies, of characters in stories, and even of their own relatives. One can well imagine that a child with such a difficulty would fail to learn to read by the "look and say" method and occasionally even by a phonic system as it is taught in the classroom. It was hoped that a picture-naming task would reveal the level of the child's facility in evoking verbal referents.

Matching by Configuration (Test 17). Rapid word matching is probably enhanced by quick and easy recognition of whole configurations, and this particular knack might make it easier to learn to read. Manipulation of whole-word configurations was measured in two ways: by clinical judgment as to the speed and ease with which the child correctly matched words (from the Gates) and by the manner in which he marked his choices.

SECOND-GRADE TESTS

A variety of oral and silent reading and spelling tasks dominated the second-grade battery. The following tests were administered. (A brief description of each appears in Appendix C.)

1. Roswell-Chall Auditory Blending Test
2. Bryant Phonics Test
3. Gates Advanced Primary, 1958, or Gates-MacGinitie Paragraph Reading Test, Primary B, 1965[3]
4. Gray Oral Reading Test, 1955 or 1967 form[4]

3. Because the present research was, in part, a validation study, the 1958 Gates Advanced Primary, which had been used in the pilot project, was administered to 301 present-study children in order to replicate the 1965 procedures. The 1965 revision of the Gates Test, the Gates-MacGinitie, was administered to 100 children who had been selected at random from the total group. Scores based on the 1958 tests were changed to equivalents of the 1965 form by way of a conversion procedure provided by Gates and MacGinitie in the *Technical Manual.* Silent paragraph reading scores throughout were treated as though derived from a single test.

4. For purposes of replicating the pilot study procedures, the 1967 battery was given to 100 children selected at random from the total group and the 1955 form to the remaining subjects. Because there was no provision for equating scores of old and new forms, both versions were administered to 50 children

5. Fluency of Oral Reading (Gray Oral)
6. Guessing at Words from Context
7. Written Spelling Test (Metropolitan, Grade II)
8. Oral Spelling Test (Stanford, Grades I and II)
9. Number of Letters Transposed (Metropolitan)
10. Number of Letters Reversed (Metropolitan)
11. Number of Words in Written Composition
12. Percentage of Correctly Spelled Words in Composition

The Effects of Intervening Variables

The quality and method of classroom teaching undoubtedly influence children's learning. An adequate analysis of these important variables would have represented a study in itself and was beyond the scope of the present investigation. However, four school principals agreed to rate and to rank the children's second-grade instructors according to their adequacy as reading teachers. A Rank-Rate Index was constructed as an admittedly crude method of evaluating the effects of estimated teacher competence on prediction.

Note was made, moreover, of the class textbooks. In some schools several series were employed, the choice of text being the prerogative of the teacher. Texts selected were: Bank Street, American Book Company, Scott Foresman, Macmillan, Ginn and Company, Laidlaw Brothers, and i/t/a/. Altogether, the most frequently used books contained many words in which the printed and phonemic patterns were discrepant. It seems probable, thus, that in most classes a phonics approach was *not* emphasized.

---

to determine the extent to which the two were related. Results showed the 1955 and the 1967 forms to have so little in common that combining scores was not warranted. Only scores of the 324 children to whom the 1955 form was administered were therefore used in analysis of the data.

Treatment of the Data

The goal of the study was to construct a short screening test for large populations.

Researchers have approached the construction of predictive batteries in different ways:

Some have simply presented multiple correlation coefficients which reflect the relationship between performance on a battery of tests and later achievement. However, as Dykstra (1967) pointed out, prediction requires more than a multiple correlation coefficient.

Others have determined percentile ranks. Kindergarten test scores and percentile equivalents are presented in the test manual, a "safe" procedure which tells how well, relative to the normative group, the child performed on the test. It does not, however, permit prediction. This fact is reflected in the designation "reading readiness" rather than "prediction" in the titles of the tests.

The procedure to be presented went farther. It used kindergarten scores to predict, by way of a "best predicting" equation, later achievement for individual children. Although this procedure is far more responsive to the needs of educators, who must identify prospective failing readers, it is also more hazardous.

In this study the best predicting equation was developed by means of stepwise multiple linear regression techniques. The method for deriving the equation can be found in any standard textbook on statistics. Essentially, the purpose of stepwise multiple linear regression is to select from an entire battery of potential predictors a subset of variables which, in combination, yield the best possible equation for predicting a criterion measure. Through a screening process, tests which do not make a significant contribution to prediction are eliminated. As a result, it is possible to reduce the number of tests in a battery without affecting the efficacy of prediction.[5]

In the final predictive equation, each of the selected predictors is weighted according to its relative contribution to the "explained" portion of the variance of the criterion test. Regression analysis permits the conversion of individual test scores to reflect the contribution of each test to reading. The sum of these single scores is the total battery score.

Predictions were categorized according to whether they distinguished between failing and passing readers. A prediction made in this way would *not* say: A child who scores "a," "b," . . . "x," "y," or "z" on the early test will be likely to score "a," "b," . . . "x," "y," or "z" on the reading test later on. It *would* say: A child who scores *below* "x" on the early test will also score below "x" on a reading test two years later.

The cutting point, "x," that separated the potentially passing from the potentially failing readers would be that point in the continuum of predictive scores that resulted in the most efficient prediction. The aim clearly was to identify as many failing readers as possible and to exclude from this group a disproportionate number of children who would succeed.

Rates of accuracy in predicting failing readers were the sole criterion of predictive efficiency. The "True Positive" rate was the proportion of failing readers identified. The proportion of passing readers who had been predicted to fail ("False Positives") was also noted.

Failure in reading was defined as a grade score of 2.2 or lower on the silent paragraph reading test.

In order to investigate whether the predictive power of the

5. The computational work for all regression and correlation analyses was performed by means of computer programs BMDO2R, "Stepwise Regression," and BMDO3R, "Multiple Regression with Case Combinations." (W. J. Dixon, Ed., *BMD; Biomedical Computer Programs.* Los Angeles: Health Sciences Computing Facility, Department of Preventive Medicine and Public Health, School of Medicine, University of California, Los Angeles, 1964 and 1968.)

instrument varied according to certain characteristics, children in the present sample were divided into subgroups according to sex, age, race, intelligence, and socioeconomic status; the accuracy of the index was ascertained for each subgroup.

Findings

The somber finding should be reported at the outset: in the group of 347 children, 16 percent of white girls, 23 percent of white boys, 41 percent of black girls, and a staggering proportion, 63 percent, of black boys had failed to learn to read by the end of second grade.

CONSTRUCTION OF A PRELIMINARY PREDICTIVE SCREENING INDEX

The Screening Index was derived from stepwise multiple regression procedures based on a heterogeneous sample of 347 kindergartners. Tests selected were, in order of contribution to subsequent reading: Letter Naming, Picture Naming, Gates Word Matching, Bender Motor Gestalt, Binet Sentence Memory, and Word Recognition. This battery identified 77 percent (90/117) of the children who failed in reading at the end of second grade and picked up only 19 percent (42/230) who actually passed. The multiple correlation coefficient of relationship between these tests and end-of-second-grade silent paragraph reading achievement was .69. The proportion of variance in later performance accounted for in the battery was 47 percent.

Analysis of the accuracy of the *preliminary* battery developed from the scores of the *total* group showed that this index predicted adequately for all subgroups save one. For the group of white girls it was not possible to achieve a really satisfactory ratio of True to False Positives.

To refine prediction, it was decided to repeat the regression analysis separately for two groups: for the 268 black and Puerto Rican boys and girls and the white boys, on the one hand, and for the 87 white girls, on the other.[6] This procedure yielded two different batteries and resulted in more precise prediction for all children. Nevertheless, the idea of offering two separate batteries was rejected as being cumbersome and unwarranted in view of the very few failing readers (14 children) among the white girls.

The decision was made, therefore, to retain and to use for *all* children the refined index developed specifically for black and Puerto Rican boys and girls and for the white boys, because it was this group that contributed the bulk (84) of the failing readers.[7]

THE FINAL SCREENING INDEX

Table 2. Screening Index: Stepwise Regression Equation for Predicting Grade II Achievement in Silent Reading by Performance on Five Kindergarten Tests

Test	Regression Coefficient	Proportion of Variance Contributed
Letter Naming	.37	.13
Picture Naming	.43	.12
Gates Word Matching	.24	.07
Bender Motor Gestalt	.28	.06
Sentence Memory (Binet)	.38	.05
Constant	.10	

The final instrument was called the Screening Index. Table

6. Some scores which had not previously been available were included when the regression analysis was repeated for the two groups separately.

7. Information regarding score range, means, standard deviations, and reliabilities of kindergarten tests, as well as zero-order coefficients of correlation between the kindergarten tests and end-of-second-grade reading and spelling achievement, may be found in Tables 1 and 2 of Appendix D.

2 shows that it included five of the six tests that made up the preliminary battery. In order of their distinct contributions to end of second-grade reading, the five tests were: Letter Naming, Picture Naming, Gates Word Matching, Bender Motor Gestalt, and Binet Sentence Memory.

PREDICTIVE EFFICIENCY

The Screening Index identified 79 percent (84/106) of the failing readers in the group of 268 black and Puerto Rican boys and girls, and white boys. The Index singled out as risks 22 percent (36/162) of the children who eventually read at average or higher levels. The multiple correlation coefficient between the tests and second-grade reading was .66. The proportion of variance in reading accounted for by the Screening Index was 43 percent.

In the group of 87 white girls, the Screening Index singled out 79 percent (11/14) of the failing readers. In the process, 32 percent (23/73) of the children who passed reading later on were also picked up.[8] The multiple correlation coefficient between the tests and second-grade silent reading was .65. The proportion of variance of later reading accounted for by the Index was 42 percent.

When the group was divided according to sex and race, True Positive levels were all above 75 percent. The Index identified 83 percent of the white boys, 77 percent of the black girls, 76 percent of the black boys, and 79 percent of the white girls who later failed. The cutting points used are those which achieved the most desirable True Positive–False Positive balance (see Appendix D, Table 3).

8. It is unlikely that in actual practice the predictive accuracy of the Index will be affected as a result of the large proportion of False Positives in the case of the white girls. Those children whose status is doubtful will be referred for diagnostic testing (as discussed in Chapter 3), and the False Positives will be weeded out.

When the group was divided according to socioeconomic status, age, intelligence, and teacher competence, most True Positive levels still held above 70 percent. The Screening Index was particularly efficient when applied to the less bright children among the black and the Puerto Rican children and the white boys (see Appendix D, Table 4). It is of interest that only four of the forty *older* white girls failed in reading.

RELATION OF CERTAIN BACKGROUND VARIABLES TO SECOND-GRADE READING SCORES

The relationship between certain background variables and second-grade reading achievement was also estimated when both were assessed at the *same time* (see Appendix D, Table 5). Of these, WISC Similarities was most closely related, with a zero-order coefficient of .53. Socioeconomic status also showed a close association: .49. Next came teacher competence: .24. The variable with the weakest tie to reading was chronological age: .14. The subgroup analyses reported in Appendix D, Table 4, provide a more detailed picture of the relationship between these variables and performance.

Evaluation of the effects of examiner experience on prediction suggested that nonprofessionals were as effective testers as were experienced clinicians (see Appendix D, Table 6). (Admittedly these coefficients are a very crude indicator of examiner proficiency.)

SUMMARY OF FINDINGS

The new predictive battery, the Screening Index, identified slightly more than three out of four children who failed in reading at the end of second grade. The battery picked up as high risks an additional one in four or five children (somewhat more in the case of the white girls) who subsequently performed at grade level on silent reading tests.

The best predicting tests, in order, were Letter Naming, Picture Naming, Gates Word Matching, Bender Motor Gestalt, and Binet Sentence Memory.

Discussion

BEST PREDICTING TESTS

The activities represented by the five best predicting tests are letter naming, picture naming, word matching (Gates Reading Readiness subtest), copying of the Bender Gestalten, and sentence repetition (Binet Sentence Memory). Three of these activities, letter naming, copying the Bender designs, and word matching, can be considered hardy perennials, and it is thus not surprising that they rose to the top of the ranks of potential predictors again in the present study.

The Binet Sentence Memory subtests have not been used in other predictive batteries. It is probably safe to say that this test reflects the child's ability to store and to recall syntactic structure. It is likely that success on this test is related to the length and complexity of the spoken sentences the child is asked to repeat. The grammatical constructions to be repeated by the child reflect essentially *adult* grammar, and his success is one measure of his ability to cope with adult grammatical units. This is the same task he faces in a primer—he has to deal with grammar that is not his own.[9]

One of the most powerful predictors is the Picture Naming Test; this test was nearly as good a predictor as Letter Naming.

9. One might note in passing that measures of syntax based on verbalizations generated by the child himself (in contrast to verbalizations in the form of sentences he has repeated) have not fared well when investigated as potential predictors of reading, whether the analysis has been in terms of traditional or modern grammars. While complexity of children's utterances has frequently shown a low but significant association with reading, rarely has it appeared as an item in a final predictive battery.

(The Picture Naming Test, though new, is highly reliable—Kuder-Richardson r = .86.[10]) Blank and Bridger (1964) have discussed the mediating function of naming in cross-modal transfer tasks as executed by children of kindergarten age. Reading, like picture naming, requires ready elicitation of spoken equivalents. Years of experience in the practice of remedial reading have convinced the author of the overwhelming importance of the ability to retrieve stored verbal symbols. The poor reader frequently gropes miserably for the words represented by the printed verbal symbols he sees on the page before him. Children with naming difficulties, incidentally, have just as much trouble learning letter equivalents as they have learning whole words.[11]

THE SCREENING BATTERY

The present study appears to have achieved its major aim: the development of a screening battery that can be administered to large populations. The index presented is an efficient predictive instrument.

The study demonstrated that three out of four failing readers can be identified at preschool level. Seventy-two of our 141 black children were failing at the end of second grade. If three-fourths of these children had been picked out as potentially failing readers and had received appropriate training early, surely that failure rate would have been much lower.

10. In an unreported aspect of the research the same measure was administered to the study children at the end of second grade. The coefficient of correlation with reading was .53, or about the same as when the test was used as a kindergarten predictor. Thus, the picture naming test appears to have a stable association with reading (at least between the ages of five and a half and seven and a half).

11. It is, nevertheless, desirable to teach the child phonics because there are far fewer phonemes than words to remember. The organization of phonemic building blocks will help him to synthesize words. However, attempts to teach phonics may fail if the dysnomic element is overlooked. The child must be provided with mnemonic devices to shore up his shaky recall.

The size and heterogeneity of the current sample have permitted an investigation of the performance of subgroups. Predictive efficiency for the various subgroups was comparable to that of the total sample. Differences between subgroups are reflected in the scoring. Therefore, the batteries can be used with considerable confidence with a large variety of children.

An important advantage is the weighting of the tests in terms of their contribution to reading. This technique should result in more precise prediction.

Administration time is short—fifteen to twenty minutes. Adequately supervised paraprofessionals can satisfactorily administer the Index after short training periods. The practicality of large-scale predictive screening for individual children has been questioned. The present research has shown that individual testing of large groups of children is not only desirable but now actually feasible.

What remains is to present a plan for using the screening battery as part of a more comprehensive attack on prediction.

PROBLEMS IN PREDICTION

No matter how good the predictive battery, it will not identify every single failing reader and it will, moreover, pick up some children who will eventually pass. The age range from five to seven is one of transition. Piaget (1967) describes the way children of this age move back and forth between the preoperational and the concrete stages. The analytic school stresses the fluctuation between the reality and pleasure principles during this particular phase. Children's performance, therefore, even from one day to the next, is less reliable and less consistent than during later years. Within a few months a lagging child might forge ahead and a precocious one might slow down. It is obvious that uncontrolled variables including family crises, extended illness, and frequent changes in teachers, all interfere with prediction.

Predictions are risky not only because of maturational ir-regularities and because of the vicissitudes of children's life situations; they are difficult also because in so many cases the situation in which the tests are used differs radically from the one which served as the basis for test development. There are often gross social and geographical variations between the base sample and new groups. For example, in certain private schools most of the children are of above-average intelligence. They will tend to score high both on the kindergarten index and in second-grade reading. Some children who score above the pre-dictive cutoff point may "pass" in terms of norm-group stand-ards but will nevertheless score far below the mean reading score *for their own group.*

Furthermore, we do not yet know the effects of stimulation by mass media on test norms. A case in point is the television program *Sesame Street,* which now reaches between seven and eight million preschool children. (See *Report on Education Research,* page 2, October 31, 1971.) One of the most important tests in most readiness batteries is the letter naming task. *Sesame Street* devotes extensive time to training this skill, and preliminary results suggest that children who watch the pro-gram at least five times a week become more proficient letter namers than their "nonviewing" peers.[12] Because the program is seen by many children, letter naming may become a less discriminating item in the screening battery; in effect, wide-scale exposure will probably change the norms, which may, in turn, reduce the usefulness of this particular test for prediction.

These hazards to prediction—that is, the unforeseeable changes over time in the children themselves, as well as prob-lems with generalization—will not be overcome so long as we rely solely on tests. St. John (1971) has pointed to the need for

12. Jerome Kagan (1971) noted that the program's implicit message that learning itself is important may have more far-reaching significance than the specific numbers and letters it teaches.

use of the anthropologist's observational tools and to depend less on "objective" or quantifiable indexes. We need to broaden our basis for prediction by including teachers' judgments and by taking into account the characteristics and expectations of the particular schools the children attend.

A Plan for Prediction

Prediction is the first practical step in the process which leads from identification to diagnosis to intervention.

The new plan for prediction provides for integration of objective and subjective data. It uses Screening Index scores in conjunction with teachers' predictions. It adapts norms, or cutting points, to the academic expectations of a given school.

Experienced kindergarten teachers' estimates of their children's future performance are known to be excellent. Teachers are familiar with their pupils and they know the expectations of their particular school. A combination of such subjective information with objective data will necessarily improve the accuracy of prediction. It is easy enough to identify children who become superior readers, and it is not too difficult to pick out the ones who are certain to fail. The doubtful cases are the ones for which a combination of teachers' information and objective data will be most helpful.

The combined information can be obtained as follows. As a first step, the kindergarten teacher ranks the children in her group according to their chances of succeeding. She takes into account her estimate of the parents' attitudes toward education, the child's attendance record, his ability to work at a table for relatively long periods, his capacity for independent work, his persistence despite frustrations, his ability to listen for long periods, his use of oral language, his interest in reading, and his desire to master it. The teacher should be encouraged to rely on her intuition even though she may not be quite sure why she feels as she does. The kind of academic demands that will be made on the children during their first two years of school is another factor she should consider.

The teacher need not be rigid about the ranking of the children. When she feels that two of them function similarly she simply places them at the same level. Once she has completed the ranking, she scans the list and divides it into four categories: children who she is certain will read well, those she expects to do average work, those about whom she is doubtful, and finally, those she feels have little chance of success. She is especially interested in this low group, but rough attempts to categorize the remaining children will help her to set apart those who are at risk.

The teacher should not administer the Screening Index to the children in her own class. Instruction for administering and scoring the Index may be found in Appendix E. In the interest of obtaining a second, more objective appraisal, the battery should be given by someone else: the school psychologist, one of the other kindergarten teachers, or a paraprofessional. Another possibility would be to enlist the services of first-grade teachers as testers; they would then have an opportunity to get to know the children they will be teaching the following year. When the predictive battery has been administered and scored, the tester should rank the children according to their Index scores.

There now exist two rankings: the teacher's, based on her impressionistic judgments, and the scores of the screening battery.

The next step is to decide on the particular point in the ranked *test* scores that will set off the potentially failing readers. Clearly, expectancy of reading performance varies dramatically from one school system to another. Suburban schools, for example, expect far more from their beginning third-graders than do schools situated in the ghetto. As a result, it would be nonsensical to use the same rigid cutoff point for academic settings that are so divergent. The method suggested here is

based on the assumption that the proportion of high-risk kindergarten children in a given school is about the same as the
proportion of failing readers at end of second grade. Defining
the cutting point in terms of each school's judgment as to what
for that school constitutes reading failure should correct for
variations among schools in terms of academic expectations.
The way to accomplish this is for each school to decide what
reading score is unacceptable in terms of its own standards. The
following is one method for defining each school's cutoff point:
Determine the average end-of-second-grade reading test scores
for the past three years. Decide upon a reading score, some-
where below the average, which would be unacceptable. The
percentage of second-graders whose scores fall at this point or
lower would represent the second-grade reading failure rate.
By determining the percentage of children who fall into the
unacceptable category at the end of second grade, each school
would establish its own failure rate. The percentage of failing
second-grade readers will define the percentage of children
who are to form the kindergarten high-risk group. For good
measure, 10 percent is added to account for the False Positives
who will be picked up in the process of identifying high numbers of failing readers.

For purposes of illustration: The June scores for second-grade
reading tests for the past three years have been inspected in a
particular school. It has been decided that a reading test score
of Grade 2.2 or lower is unacceptable. Thirty plus 10, or 40
percent of the second-graders fall into this category; 40 percent,
thus, constitutes the second-grade reading failure rate for this
school. In an upper middle class community where the average
June score for second-graders might be Grade 4.5, the principal
might decide that, for his school, a score of Grade 3.5 or lower
is unacceptable. In his case, the proportion of children with
relatively low scores might easily be only 10 percent.

In such a school, the kindergarten teacher might have
twenty-five children in her class. She would determine, allow-

ing for False Positives, the number of children who constitute the lowest 20 percent (.10 + .10) of Screening Index scores. She finds that five children (.20 = .20 × 25 = 5) constitute the 20 percent who form the high-risk group.

Let us assume that two of her children, Bill and Lucy, have ranked fourth and sixth, respectively, from the bottom on the predictive Screening Index. According to the above system, Bill belongs to the high-risk group, while Lucy has just missed it.

To recapitulate, the high-risk group has been identified on each of the two rankings of kindergarten children. On one ranking, the high-risk group has been defined on the basis of the subjective judgment of the kindergarten teacher. On the second, it has been defined in terms of the children's scores on the Screening Index, based on the school's own definition of reading failure.

The last step is to compare the two lists and settle on a final high-risk group. It is likely that the same children will fall into the risk category on both lists. There will be discrepancies, however; in these cases a conference between teacher and tester will often resolve the question of whether the child really belongs among the potentially failing readers. When the examiner and teacher disagree, the child is referred for diagnostic testing, which should provide enough information for a final decision.

Let us assume, for example, that Lucy's teacher had placed her in the doubtful group. She learns that Lucy has "passed" the Screening Index test. Reflecting on how rapidly Lucy has developed during the year after a very slow start, and on the child's genuine desire to learn, she decides that Lucy will probably make it; to further reduce the possibility that the child will have trouble, she decides to recommend that Lucy be placed with the first-grade teacher who has been particularly effective in teaching reading in the classroom. However, since Lucy is a "marginal" child, it would not hurt to include her in the risk group because diagnostic testing should resolve the issue.

The above procedures can be summarized as follows:

1. In the spring, kindergarten teacher X ranks the children in her group in terms of their potential for reading.

2. She then divides the list into four categories, making judgments as to which pupils are likely to do well, which will probably do average work, which are in the doubtful range, and which are likely to fail.

3. In the late spring the school psychologist, kindergarten teacher Y, a first-grade teacher, or a paraprofessional administers the Screening Index to the children of teacher X.

4. This tester ranks the children according to their scores on the predictive Screening Index.

5. The school psychologist, or the principal, determines the school's expected reading failure rate.

6. This failure rate, inflated by 10 percent to provide a margin of safety, is then used to designate the kindergarten children to be considered high risks.

7. The tester and kindergarten teacher X then compare lists to settle on a final high-risk group.

Evaluation of the predictive screening battery and the procedures suggested for its use reveals several advantages over previous approaches to prediction.

First, the predictive plan presents a different approach to the identification of high-risk children. The proposed tests actually predict which individual children are likely to fail in the elementary grades. Combining subjective with objective data for each child gives a far more rounded picture of his functioning and further refines prediction for the individual child.

Second, the procedures described are adaptable for a wide variety of situations. The Index itself is suitable for children from various socioeconomic backgrounds with IQs ranging from low to high. In addition, cutting points can be tailored to allow for differences in the characteristics and expectations of different schools.

Finally, the screening battery and procedures presented here raise no administrative or financial barriers to the individual testing of large groups of children. The tests require only fifteen to twenty minutes to administer. Short sessions will suffice to train paraprofessionals and teachers.

CHAPTER 3

Diagnosis

JEANNETTE JANSKY

Early identification of high-risk children is not an end in itself. The goal is prompt and appropriate intervention, which must be based on careful diagnostic study. This chapter presents a diagnostic battery offering specific leads to interventional strategies; it describes the rationale and procedures behind its development.

There are those who feel that diagnosis is unnecessary (Bateman, 1971). They object to the use of a disease model in education. They argue, furthermore, that even if it were possible to determine etiology, the knowledge would be of little help in planning for intervention. These are fallacious arguments. The approach to remediation depends in part on etiology. The child who suffers from so-called perceptual problems, for example, must be handled differently from the child with a school phobia.

To be useful to the classroom teacher, diagnosis must do more than determine etiology. It must include a careful description of the child's present status. The classroom teacher ought to participate in developing specific interventional procedures based on the diagnostic evaluation.

The question is not Diagnosis or no diagnosis? but What kind of diagnosis?

The fact is that most currently used procedures have important limitations. Children are often bombarded with a wide variety of tests—a shotgun approach—which yield an assortment of separate bits of information. The tester does not know what the single tests mean or how they hang together. For purposes of designing interventional strategies, it is crucial to get as much information as possible about the specific competences that underlie each test. What, for example, does the letter-naming task tell us? Does a child fail because he has not previously been exposed to letters, because he answers impulsively, because he confuses the shapes of the letters, or because he cannot evoke their spoken equivalents? Actually, most tests reflect *several* underlying aspects of functioning. If we are vague as to what a child's performance means, we cannot possibly devise prescriptive procedures based on test results.

A second criticism of some currently used diagnostic batteries is justifiably directed at their lack of diversity. Obviously, reading is a complex performance supported by a multifaceted substratum of competences. To be useful, diagnostic tests should capture some sense of the child's standing in several distinct areas. Leton (1963), Lowell (1967), and Olson and Fitzgibbon (1968) have demonstrated that most reading readiness batteries, which purport to aid in diagnosis, reflect only *one* underlying competence (or at most two). Thus, such batteries do not provide enough information to serve as a basis for intervention.

The third and perhaps most serious question concerns the degree to which the abilities tested are related to reading. Some elaborate diagnostic batteries study a given competence thoroughly even though it is only marginally related to the skill to be mastered. For example, it is doubtful that a diagnosis of various aspects of a child's motor ability, though in itself interesting, would be pertinent to reading. Surely some kindergarten abilities are more closely related to later performance than are others. Diagnosis must be directed to competences that are actually central to a given achievement.

Diagnostic testing should consist of a systematic and thoroughgoing appraisal. While the diagnostic battery to be described is not a panacea, it has three essential qualifications: It incorporates information about what tests measure; it is diversified; and it is relevant to subsequent achievement.[1]

Development of the Diagnostic Battery

The correlation matrix of the kindergarten and second-grade test scores of the 401 children discussed in Chapter 2 served as the basis for development of the diagnostic battery.

Analysis of the data involved two steps: (1) determining the abilities that underlay the kindergarten tests by way of factor analysis[2] and (2) ascertaining the contribution of the factors to reading by means of multiple correlation and regression procedures.

Factor analysis groups a large collection of tests according to

1. Some clinicians recommend what is called diagnostic teaching (Roswell and Natchez, 1964). This approach has considerable merit because it is possible not only to observe the child's behavior over a period of time but to adapt teaching approaches to an evolving understanding of the youngster's weakness and strength. The difficulty is that much of what goes under the name of diagnostic teaching yields a haphazard collection of single observations. After working for several weeks some testers may learn only that the child's pencil management is poor, that he reverses letters, and that he has trouble with word analysis (and most children with reading problems do have trouble with all three). Only the most skilled will know how to evaluate their findings; an inexperienced clinician might entirely miss important linguistic deficits that would make it hard for the child to use contextual cues for reading. Diagnostic teaching, thus, may fail to provide a sufficiently organized and comprehensive analysis of the child's difficulties. It looks at surface behavior while it should attempt to clarify the meaning of behavior in terms of the skill to be learned.

2. Factors were extracted from the zero-order correlation matrix by means of the principal-components method. Final loadings for these factors were determined by means of Varimax rotation (rotating only those factors having eigenvalues equal to or greater than 1.00).

Computational work was carried out by means of computer program BMDO3M, "Factor Analysis." (W. J. Dixon, Ed., *BMD; Biomedical Computer Programs*. Los Angeles: Health Sciences Computing Facility, Department of Preventive Medicine and Public Health, School of Medicine, University of California, Los Angeles, 1964 and 1968.)

what they have in common. The particular value of the method for diagnostic battery development is that the factors or abilities do not overlap, so that in speaking of ability A, one refers to a single entity rather than to a mixture. Moreover, this procedure clarifies what it is that is being tested.

Factor analysis had to answer two questions. The first concerned the diversity of the kindergarten battery, that is, the *number* of factors that the test pool would yield. The second concerned the *meaning* of the factors. To determine the latter, six judges[3] were given tables showing the tests grouped according to the factors each represented, and ranked in order of contribution to the factor. Only those tests were included that had correlation coefficients of .35 or higher with their respective factors. After studying the tables, the judges made recommendations as to factor names. The investigator made the final choice.

Assessment of the contribution of the factors to reading was the next step. This analysis involved the computation of kindergarten factor scores for each child and the calculation of their relationship to second-grade achievement. Multiple linear regression analysis resulted in an equation in which each kindergarten ability or factor was weighted according to its relative contribution to reading and spelling.[4]

The results of this analysis were to indicate the extent of the contribution of the several kindergarten factors singly and in combination.

In addition to reading and spelling, the kindergarten factor

3. Six specialists in language disorders or related fields (five diagnosticians and one neurologist) served as judges in labeling the groupings, or factors, derived from the kindergarten battery.

4. The computer program used was BMDO2R, "Stepwise Regression," as described in Dixon. The regression weights were based on raw scores in the computer program used. In a separate step, these weights were standardized to obtain an estimate of the relative contribution of each factor to the total variance.

scores were also associated with a variety of related second-grade performances not used in the construction of the diagnostic battery:[5] Fluency of Reading, Guessing at Unfamiliar Words from Context, Oral Spelling, Number of Words in Composition, Spelling of Words in Composition, Letter Transposals, Letter Reversals, Phonics, and Blending.

THE KINDERGARTEN FACTORS

The results of factor analysis are shown in Table 3. Five factors were identified.[6]

Factor I, by virtue of heavy loadings of paper-and-pencil tests, was called Visuo Motor Organization. Contributors to this factor were, in order of importance, Pencil Use, the Bender Motor Gestalt Test, Name Writing, and Minnesota Percepto Diagnostic. Factor II was named Oral Language A. Contributing tests were: Picture Naming, General Oral Language level, Categories, Sentence Memory, Auditory Discrimination, and Letter Naming. Factor III included the Gates Word Matching, Tapped Patterns, and Sentence Memory tests, each of which involved the matching of spoken or printed configurations. This ability, therefore, was designated Pattern Matching. Factor IV was called Pattern Memory. Visual and auditory activities that required recall defined this grouping. Important contributors were Blending, Word Recognition, Spelling of Two Words Previously Taught, Boston Auditory Discrimination, and Letter Naming. Factor V, called Oral Language B, was dominated by a single test, Number of Different Words Used in Telling Stories, which reflected a quantitative aspect of spoken language.

5. "Multiple Regression with Case Combinations," BMDO3R, as seen in Dixon, was the computer program used.

6. The factors accounted for 58 percent of the variance of the kindergarten tests. Factors I, II, and III each represented approximately 14 percent of the variance; Factor IV, 9 percent; and Factor V, 6 percent.

Table 3. Abilities Represented by Kindergarten Tests as Determined by Factor Analysis (N=401)

Tests	I Visuo Motor Organization	II Oral Language A	III Pattern Matching	IV Pattern Memory	V Oral Language B
Pencil Use	.75				
Name Writing	.72				
Bender Gestalt	.75				
Minn Percepto Diagnostic	.55				
Tapped Patterns			.49		
Sentence Memory		.60	.41		
Wepman A D		.52			
Boston A D		.50		.46	
Blending				.78	
Oral Language		.67			
N Different Words					.84
Categories		.63			
Picture Naming		.70			
Letter Naming		.47		.42	
Horst Matching	.39		.61		
Gates Matching			.78		
Config 1			.69		
Config 2			.76		
Word Recognition				.52	
Spelling	.43			.51	

Rotated Factor Loadings

THE RELATIONSHIP BETWEEN THE KINDER-GARTEN FACTORS AND SECOND-GRADE ACHIEVEMENT

Table 4 shows that the kindergarten factors, in combination, accounted for 40 percent of the variance of second-grade *reading* achievement. The greatest proportion of variance was accounted for by Factor II, Oral Language A (14 percent); Factor III, Pattern Matching (9 percent); and Factor I, Visuo Motor Organization (8 percent).

Table 4. The Contribution of Kindergarten Factors to Silent Reading and Spelling Achievement as Determined by Multiple Regression (N= 347)

Kindergarten Factors	Proportion of Variance Contributed	
	To Reading	To Spelling
I Visuo Motor Organization	.08	.13
II Oral Language A	.14	.10
III Pattern Matching	.09	.08
IV Pattern Memory	.05	.07
V Oral Language B	.04	.01
All Kindergarten Factors	.40	.39

Table 4 also presents the results for *spelling*. It shows that the kindergarten factors accounted for 39 percent of the variance. Factor I, Visuo Motor Organization, accounted for 13 percent; Factor II, Oral Language A, for 10 percent; and Factors III and IV, Pattern Matching and Pattern Memory, for about 8 and 7 percent, respectively.

The proportion of the variance of nine language arts variables accounted for by each kindergarten factor is presented in Table 5. Factor II, Oral Language A, was most closely related to six out of nine activities.

Table 5. The Contribution of Kindergarten Factors to Nine Grade II Language Arts Variables as Determined by Multiple Regression (N=222)

Kindergarten Factors	Proportion of Variance Contributed by Factors to Grade II[1]								
	Fluency[2] (wps)	Context Guessing[2]	Oral Spelling	Composition					
				N Words	Spelling	Transposals	Reversals	Phonics	Blending
I Visuo Motor	.10	.01	.06	.02	.00	.00	.00	.07	.05
II Oral Language A	.11	.13	.09	.09	.02	.00	.02	.12	.10
III Pattern Matching	.06	.00	.07	.03	.09	.03	.02	.05	.03
IV Pattern Memory	.04	.03	.10	.07	.06	.04	.06	.11	.06
V Oral Language B	.01	.01	.03	.00	.00	.00	.00	.01	.01

1. Contributions of .09 or greater are underlined.
2. N=158

CONCLUSIONS AND SUMMARY

The kindergarten tests demonstrated diversity in that they reflected five independent abilities.

Oral Language A contributed the most to reading as well as to six of the nine reading-related performances. Verbal Pattern Matching, Visuo Motor Organization, and verbal Pattern Memory were contributors also. In combination, the five kindergarten factors accounted for somewhat more than one-third of the variance of later reading and spelling achievement.

Discussion

FACTORS

The kindergarten tests yielded five factors. The diagnostic battery, thus, was more diversified than most well-known reading readiness tests, and much more diversified than batteries such as Frostig's, which, according to Olson (1968), yielded only one underlying competence, or at most two.

That other investigators have identified factors similar to those presented here suggests that the factors are stable.[7] In other words, if factor analysis of this kind of data were repeated, the procedure would probably yield the same factors, and it is unlikely that the factors in question are artifacts of the particular method of factor analysis used.[8]

7. One criticism of factor analysis in general and of the method used here in particular concerns just this point.

8. The Visuo Motor factor is very like the Eye Hand Psychomotor factor of Meyers, Dingman, Orpet, Sitkei, and Watts (1964) and the Strength of Closure factor (based on pattern copying) of Thurstone. The Pattern Matching factor of the present study is similar to the Perceptual Speed factor (which included matching activities) of Meyers *et al.* and the Speed of Perception factor (based on identical forms) of Thurstone and Thurstone (1965). The Oral Language factor defined here resembles the Linguistic factor of Meyers *et al.* and the

The present study demonstrated, not surprisingly, that various oral-language tests are closely related. The Oral Language A factor rested heavily on tests that required the ability to retrieve names and to pull out categories; in addition, it represented a composite of tests that measured aspects of syntactical maturity, ability to organize the relevant features of a cartoon sequence, and level of articulatory development. Furthermore, this factor was defined not only by *expressive* language tasks; the contribution of the Wepman and Boston Auditory Discrimination tests demonstrated that *receptive* language is tapped by the same factor.

It was of special interest that not all factors were modality bound. Pattern Matching and Pattern Memory included both auditory and visual tasks, cutting across modality boundaries. Because nearly all tests that made up these two factors involved *verbal* activities, it can be assumed that the characteristic common to both is symbolic functioning, which is not tied to a specific input channel. Therefore, prereading activities, such as letter naming and word matching, should probably be regarded not as modality-bound perceptual tasks but as cognitive performances.

CONTRIBUTION OF KINDERGARTEN ABILITIES TO READING

That reading is a complex process and related to more than one kindergarten factor (Wiener and Cromer, 1967) is supported by the present findings. The contribution to later achievement derives from several kindergarten competences rather than one alone.

The modest contributions of the individual factors take on substance in combination. The implication for intervention is

---

Auditory Language factor of Spache, Andres, Curtis, Rowland, and Fields (1966).

apparent: To limit remedial strategies to training in a single dimension is to reduce the probability that the child will succeed. Training in oral-language development and verbal pattern matching and memory would prepare children for reading better than would the kind of training which emphasizes one aspect alone.

The finding that, among the factors, oral language was the most consistent contributor to later performance corroborates long years of clinical experience: Spoken-language ability (both receptive and expressive) is an essential part of the core from which reading springs, and training that bypasses this important contributor will be of limited usefulness.

The Diagnostic Battery

The diagnostic battery to be described focuses on abilities underlying the tests, rather than on the tests themselves. The abilities were derived systematically by factor analysis. They are, moreover, meaningful in terms of reading.[9] It should be emphasized that all of the tests, except for the Bender Motor Gestalt and Tapped Patterns, involve *verbal* symbolic functioning of one kind or another.

9. Mann (1971) deplores the very kind of assessment proposed, in which ability testing is used to develop a profile of the child's strength and weakness. He argues that the abilities in question are reifications of abstract constructs and hence not a suitable basis for intervention. Mann points out that the time and effort spent on this kind of diagnosis might better be directed toward the curriculum. The present author maintains that diagnostically based interventional programs *are* necessary because it is quite unrealistic to expect the average teacher to manage without some kind of directive plan. Moreover, the abilities that form the nucleus of this factor-based battery may be reifications of abstract constructs. Nevertheless, test results based on factor analysis provide highly useful and practical information. Oral-language training is an example. Reading is largely a psycholinguistic guessing game (Goodman). Oral-language training enhances the child's chances for "good guessing" and is thus directly related to the curriculum. (Mann correctly points out that *non*verbal visual training, for example, is not curriculum oriented and is therefore of questionable value.)

The diagnostic battery is organized around factors, and each factor is made up of several tests. Four of the five factors that were defined in the course of the research are included in the battery. These were chosen because they contributed most to second-grade performance. The quantitative Oral Language factor was omitted because its contribution was too small.

The following tests make up the diagnostic battery. They are listed according to their factor membership and in order of their contribution to the factors:

Visuo Motor Organization
  Pencil Use
  Bender Gestalt
  Name Writing
  Spelling

Oral Language A
  Picture Naming
  Oral-Language
  Categories
  Sentence Memory
  Boston Aud Discrim
  Letter Naming

Pattern Matching
  Gates Matching
  Nonsense Word Matching
  Tapped Patterns
  Sentence Memory

Pattern Memory
  Blending
  Word Recognition
  Spelling
  Boston Aud Discrim
  Letter Naming

Some of the tests will have been administered during predictive screening and thus need not be repeated.[10] The earlier scores are simply added to those obtained during the diagnostic phase of testing.

Specific instructions for administering and scoring the diagnostic battery may be found in Appendix F. Children are assigned ratings for each test on the following basis:[11] Test scores

10. At the time of diagnostic testing, the following tests would be administered for the first time: Pencil Use, Name Writing, Oral Language, Categories, Boston Auditory Discrimination, Nonsense Word Matching, Tapped Patterns, Blending, Word Recognition, and Spelling of "Boy" and "Train."

11. In the case of some tests, score range was limited. Obviously ratings on such measures have to be regarded more cautiously than those based on tests that included more items.

that exceed a standard deviation above the total group mean are called "high," those within a standard deviation from the mean are characterized as "medium," and those more than a standard deviation below are labeled "low."

The children's ratings (high-medium-low) on the tests are entered on a score sheet in the order of each test's contribution to the factor. As the test scores accumulate, an impression of the child's standing on each factor is built up. The array of test ratings by factors constitutes the child's profile of performance on the diagnostic battery. The child's overall status may be seen at a glance on the diagnostic profile sheet.

By means of this procedure diagnosis is based on accumulated test evidence. The conclusion that a child presents an oral-language deficit, for example, rests not on low performance on a single test but on several measures of the same competence. The examiner has more confidence in his conclusions if they refer to a consistent pattern of performance rather than to the results of a single measure.

Use of the Diagnostic Battery

As has been stressed throughout, reading is an advanced linguistic accomplishment. It requires a measure of cognitive sophistication, a degree of verbal symbolic competence, some maturity of perceptual functioning, and considerable control of hyperactivity. Reading also demands a level of emotional readiness involving certain attitudes and a particular set of values.

It would have been useful to investigate statistically some of the broader aspects of the child's total functioning, but practical considerations did not permit it. Nevertheless, such variables were believed to be highly important.

To get a sense of the child's behavioral and emotional readiness for school, the test data need to be supplemented by impressionistic information. The evaluation, then, should include observations as to significant aspects of the child's behavior. The following would be noted: the child's readiness to listen and to follow directions; his ability to process information; his willingness to sit still for extended periods and to work on his own; his persistence; his impulse control; and his ability to make independent judgments. (Assessments of some of these attributes will have been obtained during predictive screening. These can simply be transferred to the diagnostic profile.) The child's answer to the question "What is reading?" is also of significance. All of this information should be included with test scores in the diagnostic profile.

The results of the diagnostic testing, fleshed out by impressionistic observations, should provide a meaningful picture of the child as a learner. In addition, the diagnostic profile should help the teacher deepen her insight into the individual child's functioning. This kind of diagnostic profile provides a starting point for intervention. Strategies are focused on the factors showing consistent patterns. Depending on the total configuration, weaknesses may be attacked directly, or they may be circumvented by exploiting the child's competences. As will be seen from case illustrations in the following chapter, all of the remedial activities—visuomotor, oral language, verbal pattern matching, or verbal pattern memory—are pointed directly to the curriculum.

The examiner is in a position to say, for example, that Lucy —the borderline child from the previous chapter—presents visuomotor difficulties and may well be slow to learn to write. However, because of her facility with most aspects of oral language, and because of her persistence and ambition, as noted during the collection of impressionistic data, she will probably learn to read by the end of second grade. Thus, the diagnostic evaluation confirms the teacher's hunch that Lucy will "make it" with good instruction. The examiner advises the first-grade teacher, however, that Lucy will need to join the group of youngsters who are to receive special help with writing.

Careful diagnosis is a prerequisite for successful intervention.

The battery presented is theoretically sound and makes practical sense. By directing attention to relevant dimensions of readiness it characterizes each child's specific and individual way of functioning. As a result, it allows for highly specific and individual interventional strategies.

CHAPTER 4

Reading Failure

JEANNETTE JANSKY

To repeat the stark facts: 16 percent of the white girls, 23 percent of the white boys, 41 percent of the black girls, and 63 percent of the black boys failed. In all, 33 percent of the total group were failing at the end of second grade. These children, incidentally, were truly low achievers; most of them could not read a single sentence. They can be expected to fall farther behind as time goes on.

Among pupils from comfortable socioeconomic backgrounds, 30 percent failed, more than might have been expected. The proportion of children in the disadvantaged group that performed poorly at the end of second grade was high: 65 percent.

There is little doubt that the achievement of the white girls was better than that of the remaining children. T-tests showed that differences between the larger group and the white girls were significant for seventeen out of twenty kindergarten tests, and these differences held for reading and spelling two years later.

The interaction between sex, race, sociocultural status, on the one hand, and achievement, on the other, is complex. Sociocultural deprivation and inadequate educational opportunities are surely primary considerations in the much poorer performance of all black children. However, the fact that white boys did less well than white girls of comparable background suggests that maleness may be an important contributor to reading failure. It is the author's opinion that if sociocultural background had been held constant the performance differences between races would have disappeared, while those referring to sex would have remained.

As for intelligence: While the children with higher WISC Similarities scores enjoyed an advantage, high IQ was no guarantee of success in reading; surprisingly enough, 33 percent of the bright children failed. As had been expected, low verbal IQ was associated with a high reading failure rate: 65 percent.

Younger children tended to fail more often than did older ones: 42 percent as compared to 29 percent. Although the relationship between chronological age and reading was low for the group as a whole, the advantage of being older was strikingly illustrated when the white girls were considered alone: Only four of the forty white girls who were at least 6 years, 1 month old at time of first-grade entrance failed in reading two years later.

In classes taught by adequate teachers (as rated by principals) 23 percent of the children failed. When the teachers were characterized as poor, the failure rate rose to 49 percent. Teacher competence seemed to make more difference for the weaker group—the white boys, the black children, and the Puerto Ricans—than for the white girls. Although the judgment of principals may be a questionable indicator of teachers' competence, the results are nevertheless thought-provoking and warrant further study. Unfortunately, young and inexperienced teachers are frequently assigned to the crucial first two grades. Furthermore, according to the principals, turnover rate among these young teachers is very high.[1] It is well known, moreover,

1. The larger issue of whether extra attention should be directed to children who show academic promise, as espoused by some school personnel, is not taken up here.

that the reading curriculum in teacher-training institutions is poor (Zedler, 1971).

Actually, changing teacher-training curricula is not going to be accomplished easily because of the lack of consensus on the nature of reading disabilities. The tendency has been to look for a single cause—a gross oversimplification. Reading failure always results from the interaction of a variety of interlocking deficits; only consideration of the child's total functioning will lead to an understanding of his difficulties. Poor performance on a *single* kindergarten test may be related to subsequent reading failure in one particular configuration but may be meaningless in a different context.

The field of reading is, if anything, more vulnerable to faddism than are other areas, and some bizarre findings have been used as the basis for elaborate and costly treatment programs. Frequently they are applied to large groups and found wanting; in such cases, the teacher's sense of bafflement and confusion mounts and may lead her to give up altogether. The resulting feeling of helplessness may contribute to the school's abdication of its responsibility to help children.

The present study suggests why simplistic approaches to prediction and diagnosis will not work: Consideration of single categories such as sex, age, intelligence, socioeconomic status, and teacher competence *is* important, but some intelligent, older children do fail in reading; so do pupils from favorable homes and well-taught classes. Obviously other factors such as ego strength and linguistic competence enter into the picture and take on meaning in interaction with the variables discussed above.

The sketches of four study children might illustrate how diverse are the phenomena that enter into reading success or failure. In each of these four cases performance on the Screening Index clearly indicated that the child was headed for trouble.

Juan. Juan was an alert, articulate boy of Puerto Rican descent. A tall, heavy child, Juan arrived wearing enormous rabbit ears. Although we had taken him from an Easter party, he did not object because he was eager for adult attention and therefore pleased to come along.

He demonstrated severe graphomotor difficulty and could barely manage the pencil or copy the Bender designs. (Two years later he would score low on WISC Block Designs—7.) He also had trouble coping with patterns set out in space and showed poor auditory memory and inferior language-processing skills. Nevertheless, he told a long story and did well on the Categories test. (At the end of second grade he scored 12 on WISC Similarities.)

The diagnostic profile showed that Juan's greatest deficit was in Visuo Motor Organization. This was not offset by solidly good performance in any of the other critical competences. It is true that he told a long story, but we have seen that the quantitative aspects of oral language (Factor V: Oral Language B) are not particularly relevant for later reading. While there were, thus, isolated tasks on which Juan performed adequately, he was on the whole a poor risk.

In addition, the information we obtained about the boy's background is highly pertinent in terms of his subsequent failure. The father had deserted and the mother was on relief. The boy was tied to and dependent on his mother, and she, in turn, pandered to his persisting need for infantile gratification. He was therefore little inclined to work, and his inexperienced first-grade teacher was at a loss how to help him. His mother refused to cooperate by meeting with teacher or principal, and her outspoken hostility was undoubtedly communicated to Juan. By the time the boy reached second grade he was a frequent truant. His able second-grade teacher thus had little opportunity to do anything for him. At the time of the reading evaluation Juan was very unhappy because, as he said, the chickens he kept as pets in his room at home would soon have to be eaten. He was talkative and recalled the kindergarten interview, but he was definitely not interested in work and he was a nonreader.

We felt sure, however, that this basically bright child would have responded to a program devised especially for him. He might have been helped to write letters and words. (Training the child to copy geometric forms would have been less efficient, because it would not have been directly related to writing.) Juan might have been shown how to *talk* his way to better writing by verbalizing what he was doing. Pattern Matching might have been fortified by having him observe similarities and differences between auditorily and visually presented verbal configurations. Attention would have been drawn to word parts, to whole words, and to syntactic units. Mnemonic devices, whether pictorial or linguistic, would have been used to facilitate the naming of letters, sounds, and whole words. In this manner, work on phonics and the building of a sight word vocabulary would have been pursued simultaneously. In this particular case, in view of the boy's need for adult attention, a great deal would have depended on the quality of his relationship with the teacher, or, better still, with a tutor who would have worked with him individually.

Sally. Sally's reputation preceded her. Her pleasant and very young kindergarten teacher told us that in the course of the entire kindergarten year Sally had never been heard to speak to any adult. We learned that very occasionally she would whisper to other children. The teacher frankly thought it would be a waste of time to test her. However, Sally, a pretty black girl, was quite ready to come and smiled in a friendly way. At first she remained mute, though she nodded in answer to questions. We suggested that she whisper to us, as she did to her classmates, and Sally was willing to try.

Testing showed that her reluctance to talk was related to her severe oral-language deficit. Her memory for sentences was poor, her ability to discriminate between similar-sounding words was inferior, her word-finding difficulties were massive, and the stories she told were fragmented and short. However, she managed the pencil well, copied designs nicely, and was moderately proficient at matching and spelling words previously taught. Sally's strengths clearly fell in the Visuo Motor and verbal Pattern Memory areas. There was no doubt as to her marked weakness in Oral Language and in verbal Pattern Matching, both crucial for reading.

When we visited Sally's school two years later, we were informed that she was vicious and had recently attempted to strangle another child. Again, Sally was quite ready to come for evaluation; although she was not hostile to the examiner, she was disinterested in the tests and put forth very little effort. Her pattern of successes and failures was similar to that observed during the kindergarten visit. She was a nonreader.

A staff member told us that Sally's mother had deserted the family. The child was cared for by her father, a policeman, who was deeply interested in his daughter and concerned about her problems. He had sought help from the school repeatedly.

We felt that even under more favorable circumstances Sally's oral-language deficits were so severe that on first-grade entrance she would not have been ready to cope with printed language. Unfortunately, the circumstances were by no means favorable. Sally must have felt angry and bereft by her mother's desertion, and the inadequacy of her verbal tools reinforced her tendency to act out. Her aggression, in turn, alienated her teachers, and as a result she was given less help than other children, while she needed far more.

In Sally's case an early educational approach might have used her graphomotor strength and her good pattern memory for learning. She might have been taught to spell certain words; drawing pictures of what they represent would have facilitated recall. At best it would have been difficult for her to move on to contextual reading. The teacher might have written short sentences referring to Sally's own experiences. She would have copied these, memorized them, and then learned the words as sight words in different contexts. To help her remember the words she would have been encouraged to recall how the original *sentence* looked and sounded. Because Sally showed absolutely no aptitude for an analytic approach, initial learning by way of phonics was contraindicated. A modified phonics approach, one based on larger phonemic segments, such as sound families, might well have been attempted later on—only, however, after the child had made a real start in context reading.

In view of her massive oral-language deficit, it would have been essential to work on all aspects of oral communication. Learning to verbalize her feelings would have alleviated her tendency to act out.

Bob. Bob, a strong, handsome boy of Italian descent, was highly proficient in using the pencil and demonstrated excellent ability to manipulate nonverbal patterns. However, he consistently performed poorly on verbal tests, whether these required management of printed or spoken language. He said little.

Like Sally, Bob demonstrated excellent Visuo Motor ability. His Oral Language tools were better than hers, though they were not really good; his verbal Pattern Matching and verbal Pattern Memory skills were inferior.

When seen as a second-grader, he was clearly depressed about his inability to read and spell. His manner changed dramatically when he was asked to attempt the WISC Block Designs; he became an alert and confident boy. On that test his score of 17 was the highest among the nearly one hundred second-graders seen at his school. His score of 11 on the WISC Similarities subtest confirmed the fact that he was bright.

We discussed our findings with the guidance counselor, who was startled to learn of Bob's outstanding performance on Block Designs. She had regarded him as somewhat slow. She volunteered, however, that one of Bob's brothers did very well in math and science but lagged in reading. The other brother was a notably poor speller. Bob's father was a carpenter. It was a closely knit family, and although the father worked with the boys on projects, it was the counselor's impression that there was little verbal interaction.

In contrast to the preceding two cases, Bob was neither a rejected nor a deprived youngster. The information obtained suggested a family history of difficulty with spoken and printed language. In Bob's case, poor reading seemed to be related primarily to inferior verbal tools; this deficit had been strikingly evident when he was in kindergarten. Because the public school system did not provide remedial reading before the third grade, he had not received the help he needed. Therefore, Bob failed in spite of his better-than-average intelligence and favorable home circumstances.

Al. This unkempt, dirty, but handsome boy, the son of Sephardic Jews, seemed to be totally unprepared for first-grade entrance. With a December birthday he was chronologically far too young for first grade. Though friendly and willing, he could not seem to address himself to work. He fared best when sitting on the examiner's lap, but even then he was extremely inattentive. He could scarcely hold the pencil. His copies of the Bender Gestalten were easily the worst in the study because of their lack of cohesiveness and his inability to grasp the essence of the designs. Al's performance on the tests was discouraging. He had great difficulty matching words and could not seem to learn to retain the ones taught him. He was slightly more successful at some of the auditory verbal tasks—at sentence repetition. The stories he told about the cartoon sequences were very acceptable and accounted for his single good test score. Thus, while Al's Oral Language performance was fair, verbal Pattern Matching, verbal Pattern Memory, and Visuo Motor performances were downright inferior. We believed that this deficit, in combination with immaturity in all areas, would be disastrous in terms of reading, and we were sure that Al would be unable to manage more than a primer by the end of second grade.

When seen two years later, however, Al was physiologically

more mature and much less infantile psychologically. It seemed incredible that he had learned to work independently. He scored at beginning second grade in oral reading and in spelling, and his silent reading score was marginal. He had failed, but he had made a solid start and his foundation was excellent. Readministration of some of the kindergarten tests showed persistence of early form-copying difficulties. Nevertheless, his ability to discriminate between similar-sounding words had improved, and he had become proficient at blending parts of words.

Al's progress in the face of tremendous odds was truly astonishing. His background could hardly have been more pathological. At the time of kindergarten testing his mother was in a mental institution. His brothers had been frequent truants and were regarded as incorrigible. Later on, they and their father were imprisoned a number of times for sexual offenses, assault, and robberies.

Al's school was the most high-powered of those in the study. He was fortunate in having superb first- and second-grade teachers. The latter reported that she and her predecessor had spent a great deal of time exploring different approaches in order to find those that would "work" for Al. By using an auditory method they had capitalized on his strength. Both had worked with him intensively on a one-to-one basis. His teacher said, "We were determined to do the best we could for him." For Al, school must have been the one place in which he felt nurtured and protected. It was obvious at a glance that he had made a maturational jump, but even so he could not possibly have managed without the devoted support and expertise of his teachers. It should be added that Al was fortunate to be the only one in his class who needed such intensive help and that his teachers did not have to contend with several children whose difficulties were as severe as his. Even so, we wondered how he would fare on the long run.

The description of some individual children has, it is hoped, demonstrated that reading performance is related to a multiplicity of interacting variables: the sociocultural background, the family cohesiveness, the academic setting, the teacher's competence, the child's genetic endowment, and his ability to cope. Any of several combinations of deficits can lead to reading failure. Conversely, various combinations of strengths will enable the child to compensate for marked deficits. Even massive perceptuomotor difficulty can be offset by superiority in the verbal area. While disturbing family problems are bound to interfere with academic functioning, there is always the occasional child who finds refuge at school and who uses learning to protect himself from outer and inner turmoil. Structured settings, as long as they are not rigid, support ego development. In children who succeed against odds one usually finds a devoted teacher or tutor who serves as model.

The educational approaches described in the case studies represent only some more or less unorthodox procedures for teaching children with very special problems. Teaching must be tailored to the individual child's diagnostic profile. No child should be locked into a rigid system, made to learn at a predetermined rate, or forced to master a particular textbook series. As a matter of course all remedial programs should be redesigned at each stage and adapted to each child's changing needs.

Innovative approaches are feasible only with an inventive and flexible teacher who will neither ignore nor reject the child and who will not stand by passively, declaring that he will grow out of his problem. Her confidence in the child's ability to learn will be experienced by him as a confirmation of his basic intactness, and each small successful step will prove it. The teacher will transmit to him the assurance that he *can* learn, and she will provide the guidance necessary for progress.

Teaching should not condescend to the child, nor should it manipulate or, worse, "shape" him. The well-taught child does not ask *why* he should learn to read. He learns because complex

symbolic functioning is part of the human repertoire and because it fulfills him to do so. Therefore, the major emphasis is
on mastery and its inherent rewards; it is not on game playing,
not on finishing a workbook, not on pleasing the teacher. The
educator's task is to help the child find a way to learn; the child's
task is to realize and to enjoy the ability he feels instinctively
he has.

Reading is a complex process. This process is mastered as the
child matures and as his cognitive and emotional potentialities
emerge and become increasingly differentiated. There are
many roads to achievement. The task is to match teaching with
the particular level of the child's development and to mobilize
his drive toward mastery.

CHAPTER 5

Intervention

KATRINA DE HIRSCH

The author is convinced that the ability to learn does not suddenly blossom at the age of five or six. Learning (and reading is one aspect of learning) rests on attitudes and competences that develop at much earlier ages. Consequently, intervention should be concerned from the outset with those forces which either foster or impede learning. The author has found in her clinical endeavors that intervention directed to two-year-olds is far more fruitful than are efforts expended after the age of four. By that time it is more appropriate to talk about remediation than about intervention.

Furthermore, to approach intervention solely in terms of techniques is simplistic. To be effective, intervention must deal with broader aspects such as timing, the context within which it takes place, and the social strategies by which appropriate help reaches those who need it. The emphasis in this chapter, which reviews present-day intervention programs, is on these larger issues.

Growth requires stimulation. Environmental stimulation is indispensable for the realization of the organism's inherent potential, as is amply demonstrated in the literature. Schilder (1964) found that training plays a significant role even in those functions in which maturation of the central nervous system is of primary importance. White's investigations (1967) testify to the plasticity of early visuomotor development. They demonstrate, for instance, that the growth of visual attentiveness is significantly affected by environmental manipulation. Infants subjected to enriched stimulation during rearing developed top-level reaching behavior in 60 percent of the time required by the control group. Young working-class children who were read to and shown picture books fifteen minutes a day presented significantly higher phoneme frequency at eighteen months than did controls (Irwin, 1960). Schaefer (1965) reported that infants who, starting at fourteen months, were tutored five times a week for one hour and whose verbal development was encouraged through friendly and spontaneous communication with a teaching adult showed increasingly superior intellectual performance as compared with others who had not been tutored.[1]

There is still much to learn about the relationship between developmental and environmental variables, but it is now accepted that developmental processes unfold as a result of the interaction between the neural substratum and environment at the time of the most rapid growth of a function.

The Need for Change

Forty percent of the preschool children—4.1 million—attend preprimary school. This figure does not include youngsters in day care centers which are largely custodial. An increasing number of preschools, however, are involved in intervention designed to supply some of the environmental nurture (affec-

1. For the effects of deprivation on the development of normal perceptual functioning see studies by Riesen (1961), and Held's thesis (1963). The effects of early enrichment have been analyzed by D'Amato and Jagoda (1962) and by Hebb (1949).

tive and cognitive) which is believed to lay the foundation for more formal learning.

Preschool education is, of course, not a novel institution. Conventional nursery schools and kindergartens, which serve mainly middle class children, have traditionally been concerned less with cognitive development than with emotional and social growth. Middle class children are, on the whole, exposed to rich and varied stimulation in their homes. A premium is placed on completing tasks and on acquiring new skills.[2] Maternal controls are not usually authoritarian—the mother tends to explain to the child the outcome of his actions, thus ingraining the relationship between cause and effect in terms of behavior and the learning of new skills. Hess' work (1966) dealing with the association between social class and the mother's "teaching style" is a beautiful exposition of these phenomena.

While a number of middle class children, for one reason or another, show marked deficiencies in information processing and oral-language development, most of them have acquired serviceable verbal tools by the age of four or five. The needs of these children are primarily social and emotional. Preschool children have a number of tasks to accomplish: They must solve developmentally early conflicts along the continuum of Anna Freud's Developmental Lines (1965). In order to be "free" for learning, children have to give up early instinctual gratifications, cope with their dependency needs, separate from home; and they must have moved toward the resolution of the oedipal conflict. They must learn to share, to fight, and to live with their

2. Social class is not the only determinant of task orientation. In an interesting study, Hertzig *et al.* (1968) have shown that even at age three there are demonstrable differences between American and Puerto Rican middle class children of comparable intelligence. The latter simply are not task oriented; they are given few opportunities to acquire mastery. The emphasis in Puerto Rican households is on social interaction rather than on performance.

peers. The conventional nursery school, whether the goal is explicit or not, must help them cope with these tasks. Stories, "pretend" activities, and doll play all assist children to master early conflicts. Interaction with their peers prepares them for life in the group when they reach the elementary grades.

Disadvantaged and middle class children share many developmental problems. Admittedly, youngsters from economically deprived backgrounds are not a homogeneous group, and a global concept of deprivation tends to confuse the issue. Horn (1970) states that individuals may be disadvantaged socially, economically, psychologically, and linguistically, depending on the particular social milieu in which they attempt to function; "they are deprived as long as they are unable to realize their potential fully or to enter the mainstream of life in their community." Nevertheless, the majority of disadvantaged children have specific and pressing needs which differ from those of middle class youngsters. It is not so much that the former lack sensorimotor stimulation—many of them are flooded with an array of stimuli which overwhelm them and which they are unable to sort out. As a result, a relatively large number of deprived children tune out, resort to passivity, or withdraw into fantasy as a defense against overstimulation. Pasamanick (1969) believes that inappropriate and excessive environmental stimulation may be as dangerous as understimulation.

What Meers (1969) calls the pervasive instinctualization of the milieu is bound to interfere with learning. The chaotic conditions in the slums and the ever shifting world the children live in do not help them curb impulsivity, postpone gratification, or sustain effort. Impulse control is a prime requisite for learning. As every teacher will confirm, children must be able to sit still, to attend, and to focus in order to benefit from instruction. Lustman (1970) relates the deprived youngsters' impulsivity to their tenuous and constantly changing relations to love objects. Life in the poverty areas does not assist children to sequence events, and as a result they are confused and bewildered. Pollack (1969) suggests that the middle class mode of viewing the world in terms of temporal succession is not universal in the American culture and that lower class Negro children may receive no reinforcement at home for sequencing and ordering their lives. Few efforts are directed to orienting them toward long-term goals or mastery. There are no rewards for tasks completed or new skills acquired.

Lower class child-rearing practices are not conducive to later functioning at school (Marans and Lourie, 1967). If one adds the physical dangers, the deaths, the violence, and the many life-threatening situations they are exposed to, it is not surprising that disadvantaged children tend to lack those ego functions which are essential for participation in the educational process.

Unlike their middle class peers, those deprived children who start out with physiological deficits do not usually compensate for their original dysfunctions (Wortis, 1963). According to Pasamanick and Knobloch (1958), "life experiences and the social cultural milieu influence biological and physiological function." This "accumulation of deficits" (Deutsch and Brown, 1964)[3] is bound to result in delayed learning readiness and in massive failure in the elementary grades.

The insistent demand for preschool intervention programs which prepare deprived children to cope with the requirements of formal education is a response to their pressing needs. The demand is reinforced by the fierce competition in middle class urban and suburban schools, a competition that has resulted in academic difficulties in a sizable percentage of even the

3. This view is not shared by Baratz and Baratz (1970), who assume a radically different position. They maintain that historical factors have resulted in a denial of Negro culture. The assumption underlying intervention is based on *deficit* models—no matter whether these deficits are viewed as genetically determined or the result of social pathology. What we are dealing with, they say, are not defects but *differences*, a hypothesis which they attempt to prove by an analysis of black children's language. These authors believe that a new model must be constructed based on cultural *differences* rather than on deficits "which simply are not there." Houston (1970) talks about the "mythology" centering around the notion of linguistic deprivation.

privileged segment of the population. The pressure for ever earlier scholastic achievement has led to considerable criticism of conventional nursery school procedures and has resulted in increasing emphasis on programs specifically designed to provide supplementary training prior to first-grade entrance.

Such programs vary widely in their assumptions regarding the causes of learning and reading disabilities.[4] Some focus on social pathology; others are slanted toward emotional and social determinants of learning. Few, if any, are concerned with the subtle interactions between organically determined deficits and the lack of biological, cultural, and affective nurture which characterize some environments. Some projects favor training for mothers; some involve the mother-child dyad, but most concentrate on the child himself. This chapter discusses some major approaches and examines some of the problems related to early intervention.[5]

Medical Screening

Birch (1968) has this to say:

Recent interest in the effects of social-cultural factors on educational achievement could lead us to neglect certain bio-social factors which

4. Reading failure frequently represents one aspect of a generalized learning disorder which may be related to a variety of determinants: genetic factors, intellectual limitations, severe environmental deprivation (both affective and cultural), brain injury or more subtle organic deficits, emotional infantilism, frank psychiatric disturbance. There are, however, intelligent and highly motivated children who fail in reading, although they do not suffer from structural damage to the central nervous system, have excellent ego strength, and perform adequately in areas not related to printed and written language. Because reading plays so central a role in the elementary grades, few interventional programs make a distinction between generalized learning disorders and specific reading disabilities. In the discussion of existing programs, the author has not found it helpful to stress the distinction between the two because they are so often interrelated.

5. Specific projects are mentioned only for purposes of illustration. Statistical aspects of studies are not taken up. Head Start and Montessori programs will not be discussed since they have been reviewed extensively in other reports.

through direct influence on the developing child affect his primary characteristics as a learner. . . . Conditions of ill health may directly affect the development of the nervous system and eventuate either in patterns of clinically definable malfunctioning in this system or in subclinical conditions. In either case, the potentialities of the child as a learner cannot but be impaired.

Interaction between social conditions and health problems is the rule rather than the exception. Prenatal virus infections such as rubella may go undetected in any milieu and may result in communication and learning difficulties in children whose mothers were affected in the early stages of pregnancy (Asbed *et al.*, 1970). Drug-induced defects are probably more frequent in the ghetto. The incidence of prematurity is much higher in the slums than in middle class environments. The consequences of low birth weight (less than 2,000 grams), which is related to prematurity, are far more severe for lower class children than for middle class youngsters. Kappelman *et al.* (1970) found that neurological handicaps of varying degrees were the main causative factor in over half of the innercity children with learning disorders. Many more children from poverty than from middle class areas are admitted to hospitals for "failure to thrive," for being underweight and apathetic, or for suffering from iron-deficiency anemia which makes them susceptible to infection. A survey in Chicago demonstrated that 5 percent of the children from deprived homes have pica and are likely to carry a lead burden that could become toxic under stress (Haggerty, 1969).

Birch (1969) pointed to another important fact: Although a child may not present a serious health problem on medical examination at the age of three, a number of signs reflecting immaturity or maldevelopment may indicate that the same child was "at risk" at a much earlier age. A case in point is malnutrition. In a field study carried out by Cravioto *et al.* (1965) in Guatemala and Mexico, psychological performance was found to be most depressed in children who were malnourished during the first six months of life. Malnutrition, Birch (1970) points out, is not a crisis phenomenon; it is a condition of life. The extent to which malnutrition is one of the significant factors in learning disorders is hard to assess because social and psychological factors independently may have similar adverse effects. Be that as it may, Scrimshaw (1970) states that children with a history of early and prolonged malnutrition tend to perform poorly on intelligence and behavioral tests.

Medical screening in the neonatal period or shortly after is an essential aspect of early intervention. Hypothyroidism, for instance, if not detected quite early, may stunt intellectual growth. Even slight hearing deficits at ages critical for linguistic development may interfere with children's comprehension and use of language and might thus jeopardize their chances for success in reading. Amplification starting before twelve months may make the difference at school many years later. We need early examinations to detect often subtle aspects of the child's functioning.

Well-constructed questionnaires might be a partial answer to the need for early detection. In 1967 M. Masland (personal communication, 1971) sent mothers of preschool children a questionnaire designed to reveal sensory and language deficits. This questionnaire identified 58 percent of 136 children who on later examination showed significant impairment of hearing and language.

However, it is not the function of this discussion to explore ways of delivering health services to children. The need is for adequate early screening procedures as a first step in the sequence of treatment and follow-up services for all significantly physically and psychoeducationally handicapped youngsters, as suggested by the Child Development Task Force in 1968.

Programs Involving Parents

Weikert and Lambie (1968) say that preschool programs for disadvantaged children which do not involve mothers are doomed to failure. "The problem is not to provide enrichment and opportunities for the children but to restructure mother-child interaction patterns." Therefore, removal of the children from their homes to more favorable environments even for long periods of time does not seem to be the answer.

In an investigation of 284 inner-city first-grade children, Goldberg (personal communication, 1970) used Wolf's scale (1968) to get some estimate of the relationship between specific parental practices and reading achievement. The association between the two was closer than that found with the usual crude indexes of socioeconomic status.

In her investigation of the relative contribution of seven maternal variables to the academic performance of urban disadvantaged children, Slaughter (1970) emphasizes the role of the mother as a teacher. Mothering and teaching, she says, go together; the child needs both if he is to perform up to his maximum capacity in an academic setting.

As it becomes increasingly clear that parental practices and attitudes are extremely important in terms of academic functioning, we note a trend away from child-centered intervention and toward work with parents. To acquire linguistic and cognitive skills, to learn to curb impulsivity, and to delay gratification —all essential ingredients of learning—children need a model. The model is the person the child is emotionally tied to, that is, his mother or some other adult who shares his day-by-day life. Thus, enduring positive changes in the child's development can be consolidated only by improvement in the quality of life at home and by changes in the people intimately associated with him.

Radin (1969) reports on the beneficial results of parental

counseling programs for kindergartners. Karnes' project (1968) consisted in teaching mothers of four-year-olds how to stimulate their children in a variety of ways. After only twelve weekly two-hour sessions, the experimental group did considerably better than did controls. In one of the most comprehensive preschool projects, Klaus and Gray (1968) emphasized intensive interaction with parents. This resulted in modification of mothers' attitudes, which spilled over into their handling of older siblings, producing what is called "vertical diffusion." Levenstein (1969) reported on a Verbal Interaction Project which had as its goal the stimulation of communication between mothers and their small children by encouraging verbally oriented play with toys and books. In this excellent project, social workers "modeled" for mothers the kind of exchange that fosters linguistic processing and age-adequate use of language.

Wyatt (1969) vividly describes the kind of mother-child dialogue which might well serve as a guide for interventional programs designed to enlist the help and participation of mothers.

Teaching verbal skills to their children, however, is no easy task for "poverty mothers," who often have been poor learners themselves. Swift, in his 1970 paper, described a "mother's storytelling" program designed to give mothers more effective tools for communication. The participants not only improved their ability to interact verbally with their children but began to view themselves as partners in the shaping of their children's development. This change, in turn, resulted in modifications of the mothers' feelings about themselves.

Programs Focused on Children

Most interventional projects revolve around the child himself. Some are based on the assumption that learning difficulties stem from a defect or dysfunction in the organism. Others adhere to a deprivation model. They assume that children fail because, for a variety of reasons, they have missed out on significant early experiences. Strategies are then devised to provide

what the child has presumably missed during his early development. Depending on the researcher's or educator's bias, emphasis may be on perceptuomotor training, on language stimulation and conceptual development, on specific prereading
techniques or on a combination of all of them.

In spite of fundamental differences in approach, interventional strategies such as those discussed by Deutsch (1967), Bereiter and Engelmann (1966), and Caldwell (1968), among others, have one feature in common: They deal with the child
directly, bypassing the parent. In the following sections a number of very different strategies are discussed, all designed to
prepare children for effective participation in the elementary
grades.

MODIFICATION OF NEUROLOGICAL ORGANIZATION

Delacato's widely publicized techniques (1966), based on his
concept of "neurological organization," will not be discussed
extensively since Masland and Cratty have taken up its rationale in a recent publication (1971). What they have to say
about the particular strategies devised for older children by the
Delacato group applies to younger children as well. There is
absolutely no proof that activities such as "patterning" in a tonic
reflex position, crawling, or creeping, combined with exercises
to strengthen the dominant hand and to enforce monocular
control, "prepare" children for learning. Anderson (1965), who
used Delacato's training procedures with kindergarten children, found no significant improvement in reading readiness
scores in the experimental group as compared to controls. Stone
and Pielstick (1969) found little to support the notion that
"neurological training" benefits reading readiness. The assumption that cortical dominance, important for language performance, can be modified as a result of peripheral manipulation
seems to be a gross oversimplification of the functioning of the
highly complex central processes involved. The reader is re-

ferred to Birch's excellent paper (1970) discussing both the theoretical framework and the therapeutic claims of the Doman-Delacato position.

LARGE MOTOR TRAINING

That development proceeds from primitive to more highly differentiated organizations has long been accepted (Piaget, 1952; Werner, 1957). Kephart (1960) postulates that motor learning is the cornerstone of this development. Masland and Cratty (1971) deal with this proposition as far as it concerns children who already attend school. For *preschool* children large motor activities, such as jumping, climbing on a jungle gym, and bouncing on a trampoline, are both enjoyable and beneficial. They help to eliminate postural tensions; they assist in stabilizing the body for performances such as writing; above all, they give children a feeling of power over their own bodies which is of importance psychologically. Large motor activities are thus a legitimate part of programs for young preschool children. It is by no means certain, however, that they contribute to reading readiness. After a period of Kephart-oriented training, Rutherford (1965) found significant gains on the Metropolitan Readiness Test for boys but not for girls. On the other hand, many children with severe motor dysfunctions are excellent readers. Cognitive functions such as reading do not depend on the level of motor development.

Kephart (1960) correctly maintains that spatial organization (and printed words are patterns laid out in space) derives from children's awareness of the parts of their bodies and the relationship of these parts to one another. Further investigation is needed to determine how far intensive body image training and the ingraining of left-to-right direction in preschool children contribute to reading readiness (see Chansky and Taylor, 1964).

VISUOMOTOR AND PERCEPTUAL TRAINING

Reading, which is fundamentally a high-level cognitive performance, requires an intact perceptual apparatus. "Perceptual disorders" have thus become equated with reading disabilities, and many interventional strategies aim at "preparing" children for reading by working on perceptual and, in particular, on visual-perceptual functions.

Basic to this point of view are two assumptions:

1. It is assumed that there is a sequence of hierarchies leading to higher cognitive performances and that "weakness" in one link of the sequence will result in failure at advanced levels. Bibance and Hancock (1969) tested the theoretical assumption that a sequential relationship exists between perceptuomotor and conceptual performance. Although the authors found some support for the assumption, the data indicated that cognitive functioning does not necessarily depend on visuomotor competence.

2. It is assumed that reading is primarily a perceptual rather than a linguistic-cognitive process. While perceptual clues certainly do play a role, particularly in the early stages of reading acquisition, they recede in importance as children get older and rely more and more on contextual and linguistic cues. Ryan and Semmel (1969) contend that language processing strategies are utilized by younger as well as by older readers during the very perception of printed material.

Perceptual activities have their place, of course. Experiences with shapes, colors, sizes, and textures are the basic stuff of living, and severely deprived, institutionalized, and above all brain-injured children may have missed out on early stimulation of this kind. They need to learn to reduce irrelevant perceptual information and to filter out nondistinctive features of configurations (Gibson, 1966). Buktenica (1968) found that performances on *non*verbal auditory- and visual-perceptual tasks combined account for 37 percent of the variance in predicting first-grade performance. According to Stern (1968), however, "The fact that a set of variables co-varies in a dependable relationship in a given set of circumstances does not necessarily mean that modification of one will produce a predictable change in the other." The coexistence of perceptual deficits with reading disorders cannot be construed as representing a *causal* relationship because both might reflect some underlying condition such as central nervous system dysfunction (Mann, 1968).

The problem of transfer of learning is an old one but it is crucial in the present context. There is, according to some investigators, no evidence that training in a serial task, such as the stringing of multicolored beads in a given order, facilitates the recall of sequences of letters. We do not know whether nonverbal perceptual training—in other words, training that does not involve sounds, letters, or words—transfers to reading. Children may improve in visual perception as measured by Frostig's tests[6] yet make no significant gains on a readiness instrument (Cohen, 1969).

The same applies to *auditory* perception. While most children have no trouble distinguishing between nonverbal environmental sounds, there are many who have severe difficulties with the perception and discrimination of complex verbal sequences, a task which requires a high level of functioning. Kolers (1969) suggests that sequences of sounds or letters may be grouped differently by the central nervous system than are nonverbal configurations. Liberman (1971), who discussed Kimura's (1961) experiments in dichotic listening, maintained

6. Frostig regards difficulties with eye-hand coordination, figure-ground organization, form constancy, position in space, and spatial relationships as being separate and distinct entities and as being implicated in reading failure. Olson (1968), in a summary of factorial studies, came to the conclusion that the Frostig tests measure a single dimension—perceptual maturity—rather than five dimensions.

that sounds do not range on a single continuum from simple environmental noises to speech. Training in identification of nonspeech noises does *not* improve speech perception and discrimination; processing of speech goes on in a different part of the brain.

The study of amounts and kinds of transfer in preschool tasks is recommended. Until we know more about transfer, the sale of heavily advertised packaged perceptual material offered for "preventive" programs is premature, to say the least. In general, children learn what they are taught, and training in perception and discrimination is most effective if it is directly related to the reading task (Weintraub *et al.*, 1971). It is at the *verbal* level that training seems to be most useful. Tracing, copying, and naming large letter forms is more helpful than copying nonverbal patterns. Cawley (1968) uses series of verbal stimuli, graded from simple to complex, to teach discrimination in the auditory sphere.

Luria (1961) has shown that the incorporation of verbal symbols into perceptual experience allows the child to generalize and stabilize his perceptions. Naming the letters facilitates the recall of letter shapes.

It is of course true that quite different strategies, including nonverbal perceptual training, may result in improved attention and more task-oriented behavior. One intrinsic benefit of such training is the necessity to listen and to process information provided by the teacher's directions. We do not really know whether it is the content of what is taught or the modification of attitudes, that is, ability to postpone gratification and to invest energy in a distant goal, which contributes more to learning.

ORAL-LANGUAGE TRAINING

Ontogenetically, mastery of spoken language precedes mastery of its graphic forms. Most children have acquired a complex linguistic code by the time they are five years old.

Difficulties with oral language have long been linked to reading failure. Ability to identify, classify, store, and recall verbal information, to select pertinent clues, and to activate output channels is an essential aspect of *receptive* language. A rich vocabulary, a variety of linguistic options, the ability to generalize syntactic rules, a large store of meanings—all pertain to *expressive* language.

If linguistic competence contributes consistently to reading prediction, as shown by Jansky in the preceding chapter, it stands to reason that deficits in this area will be reflected in academic performance.

Reading difficulties related to linguistic weakness are by no means limited to deprived populations. Mason (1967–68) found that only nine out of fifty-one speech-defective children in Edinburgh in social class 1 and 2 made a good start in reading. Linguistic deficits are, however, particularly glaring in disadvantaged children. Their frequent difficulties in processing complex verbal information, their restricted choice of syntactical forms, their limited ability to shift frames of reference, their difficulty with temporal dimensions[7]—all interfere with academic learning, which is primarily concerned with the handling of verbal and numerical symbols.

It is, of course, essential to distinguish between linguistic *differences* and linguistic *deficits* (see Cazden's publications). It is not justified to apply developmental norms standardized on middle class children to youngsters who use a nonstandard dialect or who come from foreign-language backgrounds. What counts in the last instance is communicative competence, no matter in which linguistic code.

Nevertheless, many disadvantaged children do not exploit the full potential of language (Labov, 1967). Their action *con-*

---

7. LeShan (1952) said that time orientation varies with social class, perhaps because deprived individuals have no future, literally and figuratively.

cepts may be the same as those of middle class youngsters, but they may be deficient in labeling them. It has been said that at the age of five, deprived children are one to two years retarded linguistically (Jeruchimowicz *et al.*, 1971). According to Lawton (1968), "Linguistic underachievement is a cumulative deficit, i.e., it is a disadvantage which generates a vicious circle of difficulties increasing in magnitude as school progresses." A reflection of recent concern with linguistic deficits is the rapid growth of language-oriented programs, differing widely in scope, depth, and sophistication, but all designed to prepare children for the reading task ahead of them.

A survey of such projects, the majority directed to young disadvantaged children, suggests that the programs can be placed along a continuum with unstructured approaches at one end and highly structured ones at the other.[8] This continuum refers not only to formal organization but to content as well. The most structured programs are those which focus exclusively on formal linguistic training, place heavy emphasis on cognition, and often include reading and other academic activities in the curriculum.

Minuchin and Biber's program (1968) probably best illustrates the teaching approach at the unstructured end of the continuum. They stress young children's growth in social, emotional, and intellectual areas, which are believed to develop concomitantly. Like the best traditional nursery schools, their program provides for expansion and enrichment of the child's total world. Teachers offer the children verbal tools that are meaningful in terms of their immediate interests and needs. It has been claimed that this model is inappropriate for deprived children, who need a more specific and direct attack on reading

8. The word *structure* as used in this context refers to an approach which imparts a body of linguistic information in a fairly compact form, leaving little room for essential but noncognitive aspects of experience. (See the monograph on language remediation in the disadvantaged child, edited by Brottman, 1968.)

readiness. Minuchin herself admits that strategies such as hers require multiple criteria and cannot be adequately evaluated by measuring increases in IQ. Nevertheless, it is likely that her approach significantly contributes to the child's enjoyment of learning, even if this contribution cannot be converted into conventional scores.

In the pioneer program of the Institute of Developmental Studies (Deutsch, 1965a) there is much greater emphasis on prereading and cognitive activities than is the case in the traditional nursery school, but these activities are carried out within the framework of an enriched environment. It is in this setting that training in visual and auditory discrimination and in oral language and concept formation is undertaken. The children are started at nursery school age and carried into the third and fourth grades. This "Follow-Up" project offers a highly desirable and seldom found articulation between preschool enrichment programs and the elementary school curriculum. Leaving children with severe deficits to the mercy of elementary teaching methods makes no allowance for their specific needs.

Probably the best-known and the most frequently copied of the very highly structured models is that of Bereiter and Engelmann (1966), which teaches English as a second language to disadvantaged children. Bereiter and Englemann conceive of learning disabilities as language deficits and they drill the children in the use of English forms.[9] They assume that the language of culturally deprived youngsters is "a basically non-logical mode of verbal behavior which lacks the formal properties necessary for the organization of thought." (This might imply to the children that their own language is an undesirable mode of expression, which, in the eyes of most middle class teachers,

9. Those programs which deal with interventional strategies for children from foreign-language backgrounds are not discussed here. See Horn's papers (1966, 1970), and also Horner and John (1970). For a summary of studies see the annotated bibliography of 114 references compiled by Rosen and Ortego, published by IRA (1969). See also Zintz (1971).

it probably is.[10]) Bereiter and Engelmann provide highly organized and patterned language instruction combined with the teaching of elementary number concepts and early reading training. Positive and negative reinforcers are used liberally.

Englemann (1970) states that the aims of the program are highly specific and that the content of what is being taught— such as blending—is directly geared to the goal of first-grade reading performance. Furthermore, the children are expressly taught the kinds of behaviors expected in the elementary grades—a training which undoubtedly makes them far more acceptable to the grade teacher. One of the strengths of the program is the high teacher-child ratio. Short-term gains are reported to be substantial. The mean IQ of the experimental group rose impressively; results of reading and arithmetic tests far outstripped the national norm.

Weikart suggests that "the magic of programmed approaches is almost purely illusory." (Report to the National Leadership Institute in Early Childhood Development in Washington, D.C., October 1971, p. 11.) It is true that Weikart's group consisted of intellectually subnormal and/or culturally different children. However, Weikart quotes Miller, who maintains that children taught by a programmed method and then entered in regular classrooms performed at the lowest level of any group, including the controls. In fact, Miller concluded that the Bereiter-Engelmann approach was a disaster if readiness scores are predictive of achievement in first grade.[11]

It is of interest to speculate about the reasons for these results. The following are offered tentatively: (1) Because the children were trained in all of the subskills important for reading, they

10. Blodgett and Cooper (1971) reported that one-third of elementary teachers canvassed in Alabama viewed black dialect as an underdeveloped, undesirable manner of speaking. Over two-thirds suggested that the school provide special help for children speaking a dialect.

11. L. B. Miller, *et al.* "Experimental Variations of Headstart Curricula: A Comparison of Current Approaches." Progress Report No. 9, Psychology Department, University of Louisville, Louisville, Kentucky, 1971.

would necessarily do well on tests of reading achievement. Zimiles (1968) says that one of the ways to achieve large gains is to design a program patterned after the content of the post test. (2) According to Kohlberg (1968), decoding and numerical transactions can be promoted by training children to make simple discriminations and to tie associations to verbal labels. Bereiter's and Engelmann's success in furthering children's academic performance rests on this kind of learning. In a revealing paper (1970) Bereiter explains that he is attempting to "reduce the thinking load" on children and adds that in a society in which technology assumes an increasingly prominent place the need to "figure out" becomes more and more subordinated to learning how to use equipment. He pleads for what he calls "greater pluralism" in our schools; that is, he advocates that most educational systems "avoid putting unnecessary thinking difficulties into the path of learning," presumably in the hope that the individual who has been programmed in this way will be a useful servant (and hopefully a nonthinking one) of the technological society! One will have to admit, in all honesty, that even in the middle and upper middle class there are indeed a substantial number of children who suffer because they are forced to pass through an educational system which makes excessive demands on their ability to handle abstractions. They would be happier and probably more effective in less demanding settings. This is equally the case, and perhaps more so, for disadvantaged youngsters who have been deprived of experiences which are assumed to be a prerequisite for abstract functioning. And it is true above all for those who begin life with physiological deficits. To suggest, however, as Bereiter does, that deprived children as a group should be exposed primarily to associational and rote learning, such as he offers in his program, and should be spared "the burden of thinking" has ominous social and political implications.

Englemann (1970) and his team expressly state that they are not interested in long-term gains because of the many intervening variables. But the fact is that only long-term gains count. Only these will result in a passionate involvement in intellectual pursuits, a goal which clearly is not Englemann's primary concern.

Bereiter and Engelmann, who insist on standard English forms, have been severely criticized on other grounds as well. Moskovitz (1968) claims that they use a simplistic approach to a complex problem and that their strategies rest on several erroneous assumptions. One of them concerns the relationship between thought and language; another is their implicit devaluation of nonstandard forms of English, which have a structure of their own and do not merely represent a simplified and primitive modification of middle class speech. Labov (1967) quotes a little black boy who said, "If he be mah friend, ah don't meddle him," which is an "if" construction and an elaborate one for a young child. The teacher trained in the Bereiter-Englemann philosophy would presumably "correct" such an utterance and in the process reduce the child's verbal output. A final objection to Bereiter and Engelmann's methods is their failure to conceive of language as a process of vital communication which needs to take into account the child's affective needs at his particular developmental stage.

Of several studies designed to evaluate the relative efficiency of structured as opposed to less structured approaches to language enrichment, the most comprehensive one was carried out by Dickie (1968). Her design provided for one traditional enrichment program and a number of more structured ones. Training was carried out in small homogeneous groups. Results showed that *all* children who had participated in the various projects did significantly better than did controls.

Structured programs do not *have* to rely rigidly on drills, but they sometimes fail to arouse interest in mastery for its own sake and to foster delight in learning. They may, however, have certain advantages, at least for deprived children. One of the most important aspects of learning is the organization of the task. Having the teacher structure the work for them helps hyperactive and impulsive children because they have never been taught how to approach a task in a systematic and orderly fashion. The ultimate goal, of course, is to teach children to provide their *own* organization in order to achieve on a higher level.

Many teachers prefer structured programs. They are easier to teach, and the participating children tend to pose fewer disciplinary problems than do those enrolled in more loosely organized groups. Parents of disadvantaged children, more than middle class parents, also prefer highly structured teaching approaches, perhaps because they are consonant with their own authoritarian methods of control. It is not justifiable, however, to weigh the advantages and disadvantages of specific approaches without taking into account significant variables such as length of program, parent involvement, timing of intervention, and teacher-child ratio.

The *content* of linguistic programs presents other problems. Children who have not developed a basic hierarchy of classification and conceptual organization are bound to fail in learning. Therefore, most linguistically oriented approaches heavily stress what is called "cognitive enrichment," the assumption being that cognitive processing essential for reading is furthered by means of verbal mediation.

A program of individual teaching designed to foster abstract thinking in disadvantaged preschool children was devised by Blank (1968). She postulated that these youngsters' learning deficits result from failure to develop symbolic systems. The program attempted to help them with simple cognitive strategies and information processing which would presumably transfer to more complex learning situations. Promising results were obtained with a small group of youngsters.

On the other hand, Kohlberg (1968) maintains that little evidence exists as yet to support the notion that language training per se, essential as it is, will result in advanced cognitive structures and enable children to carry out "concrete operations" in Piaget's sense (1952). He feels that benefits resulting from verbal mediation tend to be specific rather than general. Ability to verbalize is not necessarily synonymous with cognitive processing, at least not in the early stages (Flavell and Hill, 1969). Piaget (1954) does not consider language a sufficient condition for intellectual operations. Vygotsky (1962) maintained that children master syntax of speech before they master the syntax of thought and that some time elapses before they can manipulate the mental operations which correspond to the verbal forms they have been using for some time. Kofsky (1967) found that training disadvantaged children in labeling and discriminating stimulus attributes resulted in greater attention to these attributes but in no greater success in solving conceptual tasks. The danger is that exaggerated claims for acceleration of cognitive functioning might lead to a repudiation of legitimate and sorely needed preventive measures.

Linguistic training cannot be dispensed with; it is, in fact, the heart of intervention. Language does pave the way for higher-order intellectual functioning. The syntax of language and the syntax of thought do fuse at later stages (Vygotsky, 1962). Many years of clinical experience with both middle class and deprived children have convinced the author that intensive oral-language training helps children to cope with formal reading instruction in the elementary grades. Fostering comprehension and use of complex linguistic structures, teaching "pretending" and the grasping of sequences of events are essential for functioning at school.

The question to ask is not: Do we need language stimulation programs? but What *kind* of program do we need? Several criticisms of linguistically oriented preschool projects come to mind:

1. Most language programs start far too late. Kagan (1969a) feels that what is needed is a language model during the earliest months of life. This position affirms the need for infant pro-

grams. Such programs would assist mothers with what Wyatt calls "mutual feedback" (1969). Friedlander (1968) has demonstrated that an enormous amount of learning goes on during the seemingly passive listening of babies. Learning to make order out of the "buzzing confusion" that surrounds them, trying to sort out the innumerable acoustic and linguistic signals that impinge on them, is a tremendous task for the as yet immature organism. During the course of their development, children become sensitive to successively different aspects of their language environment. By the age of four, many children have learned *not* to listen and in some cases it might be too late to teach them. Maynard (1970) believes that at age four linguistic intervention is remedial rather than preventive and that success tends to be limited.

2. Many programs stress linguistic output at the expense of input. A number of children who arrive in first grade are unable to process any but the most simply constructed sentences. Their ability to understand nouns and verbs, their appropriate use of stock phrases may hide severe linguistic input deficits, which will interfere with reading comprehension. Teachers in language-oriented programs should ascertain whether a three-year-old understands the concept of "under"; whether at age four he follows instructions when told to push the truck "backwards"; and whether the five-year-old can cope with words such as *same* and *different.* Day care personnel as well as mothers, need to be trained not only to clarify meanings for the children but in some instances to modify the linguistic inputs they themselves feed to the youngsters.

3. Most programs assume that children will learn to handle verbal tools through a purely cognitive approach, without taking into account the affective aspect of language acquisition. Words can be taught in this manner. The referential function of language is relatively easy to teach. Children may even learn to use phrases in this way. But they will not acquire the attitudes underlying communication, the investment in verbal give-and-

take, the pleasure of expressing shades of meaning. Drilling sentences or labeling objects leaves little room for what Cazden (1971) calls the sheer enjoyment of the "combinatorial" use of words. There is evidence that articulation has been over-stressed in some programs; it often takes care of itself as the child grows older. Gleason (1967) has demonstrated that grammar is largely resistant to correction until the child reaches a certain level of linguistic maturity. However, storytelling, role playing, puppetry, dramatization, all of which are highly affectively colored, stimulate language and encourage young children to express feelings. Learning to understand temporal concepts such as "tomorrow" or "later" will make it easier for them to postpone gratification. Verbalization of negative feelings will help them to curb impulsive acting out and will thereby foster ego development.

4. Unfortunately, large numbers of programs reject the language of the child's environment. Far too much correction of children's language goes on in preschool settings. Such correction only serves to extinguish communication. Since children use their fullest linguistic skills when talking to their peers (Cazden, 1970), programs should provide opportunities for verbal peer interaction. The goal is to enrich the child's language regardless of the code he uses. He must be given the freedom and the tools to use alternative codes and to find out which is appropriate in a particular situation.[12]

PACKAGED PROGRAMS

Many preschool programs across the country use a packaged or "shotgun" approach. These programs provide large motor, visuomotor, and perceptual activities, training in com-

12. Baratz and Baratz (1970) say, "The goal of education should be to produce a 'bicultural' child who is capable of functioning both in his subculture and in the mainstream."

prehension and use of language, and some prereading work.

For some very young children the simple fact that the day care or nursery setting represents a benevolent, orderly, and supportive universe will make a tremendous difference. In addition, those who have been severely deprived of appropriate early stimulation will undoubtedly benefit from a broad variety of activities. However, as outlined in the previous chapter on diagnosis, it makes no sense to train *older* high-risk children in areas which are only remotely related to reading. The training of such children has to concentrate on the underlying competences that are crucial to specific educational goals such as reading.

Shotgun programs do not permit a determination as to which aspect of training is productive. Stanchfield's study (1971) might serve as an example. He exposed his experimental group to many activities: listening for comprehension and auditory discrimination, training in motor and perceptuomotor skills, practice in visual discrimination, and finally specific training in sound-symbol correspondence. The experimental group achieved significantly higher scores than did controls. But it is not at all clear which facet of teaching worked. In this author's opinion, it was the training in auditory correspondence which contributed heavily to the satisfactory results.

Furthermore, children who present *specific* difficulties do poorly with shotgun programs. They need a highly individualized attack based on a careful assessment of their needs (de Hirsch, Jansky, *et al.*, 1966). Unfortunately, few programs base instructional strategies on a detailed analysis of children's weaknesses and strengths. (The Bloomington, Indiana, diagnostically based curriculum, 1967, is one of the exceptions.) Work on the trampoline for older preschoolers who have significant difficulties with oral-language processing is a waste of precious time and effort.

Programs Involving Both Parents and Children and Infant Education Projects

The underlying philosophy of early work in intervention assumed that taking children out of an impoverished environment and placing them in an enriched and stimulating one would foster emotional and cognitive growth. It was felt that the longer children spent in such environments, the greater would be the returns.

Results were unfortunately somewhat disappointing. Once children left the program, they tended to regress. (Up to a point this was also the case for programs which worked only with parents.) Lally (1970) states that it is essential to make changes in the home so as to help parents cope with the modifications in the child brought about by his experience in an enriched environment. Tannenbaum (1970) found drops in developmental scores of children who received little stimulation after they left the programs. Schaefer (1969) stated that gains made in a child-centered home-visit project began to disappear once visits ceased.

One example of early attempts to combine direct work with children and assistance to their mothers was the Ypsilanti Perry Preschool Project (Weikert *et al.*, 1970). Children participating in the study were functionally retarded black youngsters from economically deprived backgrounds. The curriculum was designed to improve perceptual discrimination, conceptual functioning, and communication skills. Daily work with the children was supplemented by weekly home visits. Close mother-teacher interaction helped the mothers to view themselves as major participants in their children's growth.

An extension of this program is the Ypsilanti Carnegie Infant Education Project (Lambie and Weikert, 1970), which shares with the earlier one the basic assumption that preventive intervention has great potential for success when teaching is directed toward the mother-child dyad. The new project postulates, furthermore, that such programs should start far earlier than do most current preschool efforts, since the essentials for intellectual growth are supposedly established by age three. The home teachers attempt to involve the mother as deeply as possible in the child's emotional, linguistic, and cognitive growth. The program wisely rejects specific prescriptions. The Ypsilanti approach is highly individualistic, extremely flexible, and tailored to the specific needs of each mother and child. One cannot but be impressed by the sensitivity and the insight permeating the authors' case description of a teacher's efforts to help a particular mother to modify her rejecting attitudes toward a baby she had not wanted in the first place. Teaching specific skills, encouraging babbling, establishing consistent controls, and modifying unrealistic expectations are fostered in the framework of the mother-teacher relationship. This relationship rests on the teacher's respect for the mother, who is made to feel that it is she who is potentially the most effective teacher of her baby.

The Ypsilanti program goals are consistent with the basic requirements formulated by Kagan (1969a) for very young children: fostering a close attachment of the infant to the mother or her substitute; instilling a sense of effectiveness and expectancy of success even on a very primitive level; rewarding mastery; and modifying impulsivity.

In this author's opinion the close tie to the mothering person is a requisite for the realization of all of Kagan's targets. The communicative exchange between the infant and the person who cares for him—the mutual picking up of clues, both verbal and nonverbal—should be another important target. The home teacher should work toward specific goals of this kind; she will be successful to the extent that her relationship to the mother is noncompetitive and based on mutual trust.

Using as its criteria the Bayley Infant Scales and some of Kagan's categories, this project shows some encouraging trends that testify to growth in both mother and child. Everything depends, of course, on the training of the home teachers, which in this case is clearly excellent. Programs geared to modifying affective and cognitive interaction between mother and infant appear to be promising. However, they need to be followed up by similarly oriented day care experiences, once the child is ready to cope with an expanded environment in which the mother is an active and involved participant.

A new venture is the Family Day Care Program in the Richmond, Virginia, area (Crawford, 1970), a free service to mothers needing day care for toddlers who cannot or should not be absorbed in a group. This program consists in care by the day in the home of a neighboring family. In many cases it serves as a substitute for foster home placement, thus allowing the mother to retain her child. All of the day care personnel are warm and motherly women who are visited bimonthly by case aides with whom they discuss the child's adjustment, physical, social, and emotional. Training sessions for both natural and day care mothers are held monthly and involve discussion of all phases of child development. It appears that children who were moved from such programs to day care centers showed less separation anxiety and more inclination to explore than nonparticipating children.

An interesting and multifaceted project is that of Lally (1970) at Syracuse University Children's Center, which combines service and research. Several interlocking projects use large numbers of indigenous paraprofessionals. The prenatal project starts with the mother *before* the birth of her child and continues as long as the child and his family are associated with the Center. Another project which includes children from eighteen to forty-two months is designated the "family style" program because children of varying ages live and work together in a setting which resembles that of the normal family. Some of the questions raised by Lally are: Do children in the combined Home-Visit-Center program show less developmental regression than those who participate solely in the activities of the Children's Center or those whose mothers only are helped? What are the advantages to the family of joining the project before the birth of the child as compared to joining it later?

In the past, intervention programs had one specific feature in common: "Experts" taught parents how to teach their children. It was the expert who imparted information and encouraged the parent to foster task orientation and better verbal communication. These are admittedly middle class goals, and it can be assumed that they assist children to cope more effectively with formal education.

Some members of ethnic communities object, however, to the philosophy underlying such approaches. Quite a different strategy, therefore, is employed by Scheinfeld *et al.* (1970), who begin with the parents' *own* value system and work from there. Scheinfeld selected a small number of children with weak ego strength from the nursery school. Interviews with the mothers elicited *their* ideas about child rearing. In other words, the mothers were encouraged to formulate their feelings as to the basic function of the parental role. They were asked to set priorities, and those which coincided with the nursery school priorities were selected for work. Participation by the mothers in the activities of the wider community was strongly urged. The mothers who were most successful with their children were those who developed a sense of their own competence.

Scheinfeld formulated the conceptual framework as follows: Parents cannot construe the child's relationship to the world in ways that are fundamentally different from their own. Hence, to change child-rearing practices effectively, one must change the parents' own experience.

Approaches to Teaching

A number of preschool programs have adopted a model based on principles of operant conditioning with behavior modification as its central feature. The approach is tied to specific tasks and seems to be successful for the acquisition of isolated behaviors and circumscribed skills (and these skills might well be important). The method has worked with retarded children who benefit by an approach which uses small steps. It does not seem to be particularly effective when it comes to integrating new cognitive structures. Growth of reasoning and language cannot be interpreted in terms of learning theory. Flavell and Wohlwill (1969) point out that the Skinnerian model, which is essentially "linear" in type, reduces learning to the question of whether the child has mastered all the steps that precede and are requisite for the concept that is to be learned. Even if he has, the authors say, the concept will be acquired not as a general one but as a separate unrelated entity and thus will not transfer.[13] There is little room for generalization, which is ultimately at the heart of all learning.

The principle of operant conditioning, with its emphasis on immediate and mostly extrinsic reinforcement, has been objected to because of its molecular view of human learning. Learning does not consist in the acquisition of separate facts. Even at early stages learning is primarily concerned with the ability to form hypotheses, to weigh evidence, and to draw inferences.

The principle of teaching very circumscribed and specific skills is operative also in programmed instruction and teaching machines (Jackson, 1968). According to Lumsdaine (1961), programmed instruction "creates an essentially reproducible sequence of instructional events and accepts responsibility for efficiently accomplishing change."

While the art of programming is, theoretically at least, an extension of the art of teaching (Bruner, 1963), and while some

13. Stimulus-response theories, according to Goodman (1972), view learning as an accumulation of bits and pieces and break it down into sequences of small tasks, while in reality this is not the way children learn to read.

brilliant programs expose children to far better instruction than that offered by a mediocre teacher, there are nevertheless dangers. The very fact that programmed instruction accepts "responsibility for learning"—that, in other words, it fosters passivity—is by no means an advantage, as anyone who has worked with intelligent and passive children can testify. Teaching is not a matter of pouring information down a child's throat. Learning is, ultimately, an aggressive act.

Programmed instruction, moreover, precludes the spontaneous interaction between teacher and pupil which fosters a sense of excitement and discovery (Schiff, 1971). No teaching machine is able to say, "I don't know the answer to that one, but let's try to see if we can work out a solution together."

Winsberg (1969) came to the conclusion that controlled studies have so far failed to demonstrate any clear-cut superiority of programmed instruction over traditional classroom methods. This author has not found the use of teaching machines helpful in the case of pupils who present severe and specific reading difficulties and who require not only highly sophisticated techniques but also the constant support of an understanding tutor. Such support is a more powerful agent than any extrinsic reinforcer could be. Jackson says that while the machine can store countless bits of information it will never *know* the pupil, and it is quite true that only the living teacher can exploit the child's interests and preoccupations in the service of the learning goal. Only through an attachment of this kind can some children become involved in academic pursuits (Eckstein and Motto, 1969).

Internalizing a devotion to and excitement about learning is a complex phenomenon that has its roots in the child's early life. (See Kagan's work and the psychoanalytical literature.) It is fostered by identification, which is a far more subtle and encompassing mechanism than is operant conditioning. Identification implies a desire on the part of the learner to internalize not only single elements but the basic attitude of the model. It also implies that this attitude does not remain a foreign body, as it were, but is integrated in the learner's way of meeting the world and thus becomes part and parcel of his internalized value system. Identification helps the child to make the transition from the "pleasure" to the "reality" principle and enables him to carry on even when the going is rough. In the beginning, the adult with whom the child identifies "lends" him his delight in mastery, his desire to do well, and his pride in achievement. In the case of deprived youngsters, it is difficult to conceive how a mechanical device that eliminates the very thing they need most, the support of an understanding adult they can trust and identify with, could be conducive to learning.

Identification is, of course, easier to achieve in a one-to-one relationship than in a classroom (although a gifted teacher will lend herself as a model to very different kinds of children). Because identification has its genetic roots in the child's attachment to the mothering person, the use of "substitute mothers" in day care centers, especially for very young children, is a matter of some urgency.

Palmer (1968) found that young children who were simply played with individually made as much progress as did others who received individual "intellective" training. He concluded that the gains made by both groups were based on the affective and cognitive interaction between the tutor and the individual child and that "*Any* well conceived and structured program may well have equally beneficial results, provided it is introduced early enough in the child's life and an unencumbered one-to-one relationship occurs . . . over an extended period of time."

Even in older children attention improves, impulsivity diminishes, and anxiety is reduced in the presence of a warm and understanding teacher. On the basis of a trusting relationship, he can make realistic demands on the pupil, who experiences them not as an increase in pressure but as an expression of the adult's trust in and respect for his ability to perform.

Timing of Intervention

The question of the optimal time for intervention is an urgent one. The following issues need to be raised: Does early experience provide the foundation on which later learning rests? Is severe deprivation at young ages irreversible? Can deprivation be compensated for?

The quality of early experience crucially affects development, and, with time, it becomes more and more difficult to compensate for accumulated deficits (Ausubel, 1966; Bloom, 1964; Goldfarb, 1945). Hunt (1964) feels that adverse environments are most likely to inhibit growth—and specifically growth of language in the years following infancy.

Birch (1969) maintains that learning is not simply a cumulative process and that interference at specific times may result in disturbances of function that are both profound and of long-term significance. It is the correlation of the experiential opportunity with a given stage of development which is crucial. Certain basic skills underlying higher-level tasks are possibly more easily generalized at earlier than at later ages (Feldmann *et al.*, 1968). In order to clarify the issue, we need detailed phenomenological observations of what happens between infancy and age three. The psychoanalytic school has collected a host of data related to early psychosexual development. Studies now being carried out at Harvard (Pines, 1969) are geared more toward behavioral information. We have to learn far more than we know now about the sequence of early physiological, affective, and cognitive events and the specific ways they interact.

That absence of sensorimotor and affect stimulation is detrimental to growth was shown by Provence and Lipton (1962). Ability to identify probably develops very early in the child's life. Children who are not fondled and cherished and who have failed to make a meaningful attachment to a mothering person may become apathetic and unable to learn. The foundations for comprehension and use of language are laid far earlier than was previously assumed. Language learning depends not only on the neural mechanisms involved and on inherent maturational processes but also on the mother's affect and verbal interaction with the child and, as time passes, on her "teaching style." Because sensorimotor schemata essential for subsequent cognitive functioning develop during the first two years of life, the feeling today is that intervention cannot start too soon.

In fact, because many young mothers resist counseling even if it is available, steps may have to be taken in some cases to prepare mothers for interaction with the worker before the baby is born. The trained home visitor can make herself useful to the pregant mother by obtaining medical or legal help should she need it. On the basis of this kind of practical relationship the worker may be able to alleviate feelings of dread and despair associated with the impending birth of a child the mother may not have wanted in the first place. The worker can thus facilitate the forming of affect bonds between the mother and her baby—bonds which are essential for the infant's physical and emotional survival. Once the mother is on comfortable terms with the worker, she will be more inclined to accept suggestions, should there be need for early intervention.

Designs and Evaluations of Programs

Valid objections to present-day evaluation procedures have been raised. Many projects use scores on the Stanford-Binet or the Illinois Test of Psycholinguistic Abilities (ITPA) as their criterion for change. However, the practice of formal testing to estimate a child's status has been questioned for some time. Labov (1969) demonstrated the degree to which deprived children's performance is influenced by fear and suspicion of adults who belong to a different culture and whose communicative style is foreign to their experience. Not only the cultural background but the individual style of the examiner may make a notable difference in test results. Thomas *et al.* (1971) demonstrated that WISC scores of Puerto Rican children were significantly affected by differences in the individual approach of examiners who were of the same sex and ethnic background and who were equally fluent in both English and Spanish. Higher performance was elicited with examiner behavior that encouraged active participation, verbalization, and sustained effort on the child's part.

As regards the instruments themselves, Zimiles (1968, 1970) believes that the WISC, the Stanford-Binet, and the ITPA provide only limited information about the cognitive processes which mediate children's intellectual functioning. In the place of absolute evaluations dominated by psychometric techniques he suggests "operational" procedures which assess the degree to which subgoals have been reached. He asks the following questions: Does the proposed intervention maximize the probability of achieving the stated goal? Is the mode of implementation suitable to the objectives sought? Are the goals and operations sufficiently differentiated according to age, developmental level, and cultural background of the participating children?

Cawley (1968) makes the important criticism that evaluations of intervention programs usually employ univariate measures in an area in which the problems are multivariate. Techniques must be found to measure children's progress in the various facets of each program.

Stern (1968) suggests that the stated goals of intervention do not always correspond with the terminal behaviors which serve as criteria. She herself constructed measurements designed to evaluate changes in specific areas of the program.

Hertzig and Birch (1971) state that indexes of behaviors pertinent to school learning may be more sensitive criterion measures than IQ in disadvantaged children. School attainment may be significantly modified even if the IQ has not changed.

Longitudinal studies are clearly needed because in the last

instance judgment as to progress must be based on *long-term* results. Some gains might be "washed out," and others might show only after some time has elapsed. Subtle changes in the child such as task involvement are unlikely to be directly reflected on tests administered only a few months after the original evaluation.

Light and Smith (1970) discuss other important issues. They maintain that researchers often fail to set priorities for various goals in their projects. The goals themselves are occasionally contradictory. These researchers, furthermore, object to the concept of "average gains" as a measure of progress for projects involving heterogeneous samples. A careful analysis of group characteristics might enable us to match interventional efforts to specific subgroups.

Light and Smith also inquire into unintended consequences of programs which might or might not be beneficial and they want to know which features are controllable and which are not. They point to the necessity of replicability. They raise the relevant question: Which program works well for reasons which are known to us and which can be reestablished in any future enterprise? An answer would make it possible to determine whether success is more than accidental and is thus worth replicating.

In the same excellent paper the authors analyze program designs now in use. They criticize the two most frequently employed *post hoc* experimental models. In both, evaluation takes place *after* the results are in. Their own "sequential" model proposes the setting up of trial centers, a few at a time. Incoming information from these centers would make it feasible to estimate which combination of features shows the greatest promise. A second round of centers would then be created with program features close to the optimum combination. This cycle would be continued until an effective project was attained.

Such a model requires time, of course, and intervention is so desperately needed that it is difficult to say whether there is enough time to try out what seems to be an eminently reasonable approach to the problem. The point made by Light and Smith is simply this: Using sequential evaluations and systematically adjusting and changing strategies according to new insights are far better than throwing together hundreds of stray variations only to reject them after a decade because they have major flaws.

Discussion

A number of theoretical and practical problems should be explored carefully.

1. Are there "critical" phases of development—Vygotsky calls them "sensitive periods"—when training and stimulation are particularly effective? Hunt (1961) defines a critical stage as one during which the organism's encounters with given kinds of circumstances are especially productive for the acquisition of new patterns and structures.

The consensus seems to be (Bloom, 1964; Lenneberg, 1967) that there are phases during which the child is particularly susceptible to certain kinds of stimulation. At each maturational stage the growing organism becomes capable of accepting different types of input which are resynthesized in a new stage. Scott (1962) maintains that development can be modified only during periods of maximal growth of sensory, motor, cognitive, and emotional structures. Prior or subsequent to such critical periods the identical experience may have different consequences, or no consequences at all. Most researchers think of "critical periods" in terms of physiological development. While it is essential to continue to explore the "biological timetable" for specific functions (Penfield and Roberts, 1959), a similar timetable holds for psychological development. At each stage the child has both a phase-characteristic and an individual way of viewing the world. The kinds of stimulation offered to the child should match his developmental needs of the moment.

2. Do long-term gains result from interventional programs? Bloom (in Pines, 1969) reports on lasting cognitive changes in an Israeli nursery project that worked with babies twenty-two hours a day at least for four years.

A University of Wisconsin project, now in its fifth year, tells of striking benefits in ghetto children of retarded mothers. A team headed by Heber (1970) provided individual tutoring shortly after birth and placed the child in classes at the age of two years. At age four the experimental group showed a mean IQ in the 120–130 range while the contrast group scored a mean IQ of about 80.

The Ypsilanti Perry Preschool Project, which followed experimental and control groups over several years, reported some interesting findings: Children in the experimental group obtained significantly higher scores on *achievement* tests than did controls. These differences persisted through the years of follow-up, *including* third grade. Participating children received better ratings by elementary teachers in academic, emotional, and social development than did controls. These differences also held up throughout the years that followed.

Results of recent studies have shown that the hope for *instant* enrichment is a vain one. The Institute for Developmental Studies (Deutsch, 1965a) has this to say: "Only by sustained, painstaking, innovative action can one hope . . . to launch children on careers of fruitful learning."

3. What size groups are most suitable for intervention programs?

Small-group teaching appears to be most effective. According to Holmes and Singer (1961), the younger the child, the greater the need for small as contrasted to large groups. There is some agreement that the smallest possible teacher-child ratio is most conducive to learning. For emotionally deprived youngsters a one-to-one situation seems to be the most promising. The author agrees with Blank (1968) that a one-to-one relationship would be essential also for rehabilitation of severely deprived youngsters who have failed to develop information-processing strategies.

4. Can cognitive growth be separated from emotional growth?

The fact is that emotion and cognition are interdependent in many subtle ways. An example might be illustrative: One Infant Educational Program correctly stresses the importance of the face schema in the development of the baby and suggests cognitive strategies for teaching it. In reality normal babies' "learning" of the mother's face is embedded in the affective interaction between mother and child, and cognitive enrichment is part and parcel of the affective flow between them.

Biber (1965) says that the separation of cognitive from noncognitive aspects of development in the early years is one of the dangers of contemporary education. In many programs for young children there is little awareness of the intermingling of cognitive and emotional streams of growth. Cognitive learning must be infused with the energy derived from the child's affects and drives. Young children do benefit from acquiring skills and from intellectual challenge. Mastery is an important aspect of ego functioning. In 1930 Isaacs demonstrated that children are probably much more ready for problem-solving tasks than we have been ready to admit for the past forty years. Nevertheless, training in specific tasks simply will not "take" if the youngster is not affectively involved in what he is doing and if the task is not relevant to his needs.

The training of specific skills is impossible if the child is so impulse-ridden that he cannot attend. It is through his relationship to a warm and supportive teacher that he slowly acquires inner controls. Thus, the emotional climate of the setting and the degree of empathy and insight into the individual child's needs are crucial for cognitive growth. We need our most perceptive and talented teachers at this early stage. Lustman

(1970) has pointed out that a continuity of affect bonds is essential, especially for children at risk. It is thus highly desirable that the same carefully trained and intuitive teachers remain with their groups for a number of years.

5. Is intensive involvement of parents a prerequisite for success?

The consensus of opinion clearly is that parental involvement is a necessity (Bing, 1963; Milner, 1951; Crandall *et al.*, 1960; Coleman *et al.*, 1966; Lally, 1970; Scheinfeld *et al.*, 1970; Taylor, 1970). How to achieve it in the face of often severe maternal depression and feelings of inadequacy is the problem (Wortis *et al.*, 1963). A sense of being in control of their own lives and the life of the community appears to be a prerequisite for parents' involvement in their children's academic progress.

6. Do middle class children need intervention?

While it is well known that large numbers of deprived youngsters lag in linguistic development, the number of middle class children whose verbal tools are inadequate is currently underestimated. Among the 3 to 15 percent of middle class pupils who fail in reading, writing, and spelling in the elementary grades, the majority present at preschool age linguistic deficits related to a variety of causes: genetic, organic, maturational, and psychological. Regardless of class, *all* children who have trouble identifying, classifying, storing, and recalling linguistic information, and whose expressive verbal tools are poor, need intensive help with all aspects of language.

7. Are our evaluation procedures and program designs adequate?

They are not. Ongoing evaluation of programs is much to be preferred to *post hoc* tests which are dominated by quantitative assessments. The model outlined by Light and Smith (1970) deserves earnest consideration.

Recommendations

There is urgent need for the earliest possible identification of children who present developmental deficits—red flags that forecast learning disabilities in the years to come. Overall planning to meet this need would require home programs for infants, family centers for toddlers, and kindergarten screening. For children who are at risk such programs should be ongoing: They should include diagnosis, appropriate intervention, and follow-up procedures.

Infant programs should be initiated as an extension of postnatal care and should provide for trained workers to visit the homes of babies suspected of being at risk. A trusting relationship between the mother and the worker, based on the latter's availability for the mother's everyday needs, would allow the worker to model ways of handling small children that best promote social, emotional, and cognitive growth.

The Family Center,[14] which a child would enter between twenty and thirty months, would be an organic outgrowth of such home programs. Here children from very different milieus would be provided with an orderly, supportive universe—one that would foster task involvement, impulse control, and enthusiasm for mastery. In the framework of a meaningful relationship with the adults who care for them, the children would enlarge their world, acquire more sophisticated communicative skills, and become involved in a variety of new experiences. Those youngsters who are vulnerable neurologically and psychologically and who present difficulties with processing and generating language would be singled out for individual and specific intervention. The mother's active participation in the

14. This manuscript was in print before J. McV. Hunt's paper, "Parent and Child Centers: Their Basis in the Behavioral and Educational Sciences," appeared in the *American Journal of Orthopsychiatry* in January 1971. See also "An Invited Critique," by E. Gordon, in the same volume.

program certainly would be at the heart of these efforts.

At kindergarten age formal screening procedures (as described in Chapter 2) would identify educational high risks. Subsequent diagnostic evaluation of children so identified would result in profiles of individual weaknesses and strengths that would make possible the devising of pedagogic strategies tailored to each child's needs.

Children who present continuing deficits at the end of their kindergarten year would receive intensive help in transition classes to better prepare them for the demands of first grade (de Hirsch, Jansky, *et al.*, 1966).

Continued reevaluation and intervention through the elementary grades would be essential.

A prerequisite for such a course of action would be the training of preschool personnel. Better recruitment, improved selection procedures, more intensive education in child development would have as their goal a modification of preschool teachers' attitudes and techniques.

Extensive training and use of volunteers, students, paraprofessionals, and community-based personnel would be a necessity. Young children's dependency needs are formidable. Paraprofessionals could learn to serve as substitute mothers, thereby facilitating the transition from home to the larger world.[15]

It is perhaps unrealistic to expect at this point a nationally supported program of this kind. The Child Development Task Force (1968) rightly recommends "model centers" for developing radically new approaches. The Task Force proposes that newly emerging features be incorporated and evaluated in a series of "demonstration centers," which would try them out.

15. Under the paraprofessional Training Project-R, sponsored by the Wayne County, Michigan, School System (1971), trainees are taught to identify potential problem children at kindergarten age. Such training could be extended downward to teach paraprofessionals to become aware of high-risk children much earlier—between thirty and forty months of age.

These nodal points would have service, training, and research functions and would involve geographically and socially divergent groups. All programs would continue to feed information into a central agency designed to evaluate the various strategies.

The ultimate goal is the formulation of a national program to give young children a chance to benefit from educational experience.

Our schools are overwhelmed by enormous numbers of children who are unable to cope. Results of remedial programs for older children have been disappointing. A radical new approach is needed. This book has outlined a plan for limiting the number of children destined to fail.

The Early Predictive Index

JEANNETTE JANSKY

In the course of the present investigation the early Predictive Index that had been developed in the course of the pilot study was evaluated.

We had not expected the early Index to emerge from further investigation in exactly its original form. It had been designed to demonstrate that one can go beyond the percentile ranking of kindergarten children according to their reading readiness and identify potentially failing readers before they are exposed to formal education. This earlier instrument combined prediction and diagnosis. It was assumed that to be efficient in forecasting reading—a highly sophisticated linguistic performance—predictive tests should reflect the child's maturational status in a variety of areas.

The Predictive Index was a ten-test battery, including Pencil Use, the Bender Motor Gestalt, the Wepman Auditory Discrimination, Categories, Number of Words Used in Telling a Story, the Horst, the Gates Word Matching, two Word Recognition tests, and a simple Spelling task. Out of the original group of fifty-three, this Index identified ten of the eleven kindergarten children who actually failed in reading at the end of the second grade.

The small size of the original sample precluded study of Index accuracy for subgroups. In the early sample the IQ range was from 90 to 116, and the children belonged to a fairly homogeneous lower middle class group. Furthermore, the sample was self-selected inasmuch as only those children were tested whose parents were willing to bring them. These limitations made it unlikely that the results could be generalized to large socioeconomically and intellectually heterogeneous groups.[1]

We were confident that by and large the *tests* which made up the Predictive Index would again show a significant relationship with reading performance. We were, however, concerned that the *cutoffs* established in the pilot study might not apply to groups that were different from the original sample.

We received countless letters telling us how helpful the battery was in orienting kindergarten teachers to observe behaviors and attitudes that make for subsequent success or failure in reading. We ourselves continued to use the tests successfully in clinical practice. We were, therefore, interested in the outcome of further study of the Predictive Index.

Sample and Tests

The follow-up study of the Predictive Index was based largely on the performance of the children described in Chapter 2. The heterogeneous sample consisted of 158 white and 124 black and Puerto Rican children. It included 146 boys and 136 girls. Altogether, the performance of 282 children was studied.[2]

The ten Index tests were, with one exception,[3] administered and scored as described in *Predicting Reading Failure* (de Hirsch, Jansky, *et al.*, 1966). The Gray Oral and the Gates Advanced Primary Reading tests, separately, were used as criterion variables.[4]

1. Relatively global statistical procedures were used in analyzing the early data. We felt that simple statistics were best suited to the characteristics of the tests and to the study aims. No attempt was made, for example, to weight the predictive tests according to their relative contribution to reading.

2. Only 282 children participated in this aspect of the research because two of the criterion measures (the oral and silent reading tests) had been administered to only 300 children. Of these, complete Predictive Index test scores were available for 282 subjects.

3. In the pilot study, Number of Words was estimated by counting the words in the children's account of "The Three Bears." In the present study (as reported on p. 166), two cartoon series were chosen to elicit stories. This alteration might have influenced the outcome.

4. In the early study the second-grade criterion was a *combined* score derived from performance on three tests: the Gray Oral Reading Test, the Gates Advanced Primary Reading Test, and the Metropolitan Spelling Test.

Treatment of the Data

The investigation of the original Predictive Index called for relatively simple data-processing procedures. It was assessed how frequently low kindergarten scores on the Predictive Index identified the children who failed in reading at the end of second grade.

In accordance with the procedures outlined in *Predicting Reading Failure*, an Index score was calculated for each child. Three or fewer passing subtest scores at kindergarten level presumably placed a child in the high-risk category. Reading failure, as before, was defined as a score of Grade 2.4, or lower, on either reading test.

Predictive efficiency was estimated on the basis of three analyses. The first consisted in determining for the 282 children in the present sample whether the Predictive Index correctly identified as many failing and passing readers as it had in the much smaller and far more homogeneous original group. In order to investigate the possibility that the predictive power of the Index might be related to sex, race, or socioeconomic background, the larger group was subdivided. True and False Positive rates were the measure of predictive efficiency.

The second analysis was based on the performance of a subsample of fifty-three children who were selected from the total group to match, roughly, the subjects of the pilot study in race, sex, and intelligence (it was not possible to match them for socioeconomic background).[5] For purposes of this second analysis, oral and silent reading and spelling test scores were combined, as they had been in the pilot study. The second analysis, thus, represented an attempt to replicate the conditions of the early study.

Finally, fortuitous circumstances provided a third estimate of the efficacy of the Predictive Index. The battery had been used in a setting quite independent of the present research. The investigator, the principal of a school in California, supplied the author with Predictive Index and end-of-second-grade reading scores. Criterion was the mean of the Gates-Gray scores. All scores were prepared by the present investigator in a frequency distribution table identical to that used in our original study. The California sample included thirty-seven chil-

5. The pilot group and the present subsample included thirty boys and twenty-four girls. Forty percent of the children were black. For the present study subsample, children were selected whose WISC Similarities scores ranged from 9 to 13 and were thus roughly comparable to those in the early study.

dren—seventeen boys and twenty girls. No information was available as to the socioeconomic status or racial characteristics of the groups.

Findings

Nine of the ten Predictive Index tests were again significantly related to reading and spelling at the end of second grade. The only measure that failed to show a close association with reading was Number of Words. (Pencil Use proved to be important for spelling.)

In describing each of the three follow-up groups—the large heterogeneous sample, the matched subsample, and the California sample—the findings from the present investigation will be compared with those of the early study.

THE HETEROGENEOUS GROUP

In the pilot study the Predictive Index had yielded a True Positive rate of 91 percent and a False Positive rate of only 10 percent. By contrast, in the present investigation, when a cutting point of 3 or lower on the Predictive Index tests was used to indicate subsequent reading failure, the Index picked up only 32 percent (34/108) of the failing readers. When this cutoff score was set at 6, the Index correctly identified at kindergarten level 77 percent (83/108) of the children who failed reading at the end of the second grade. With the higher cutoff score, the Index also picked up far too many of those who eventually passed—35 percent (60/174). Therefore, the Predictive Index was judged to be less efficient for an unselected group of children from heterogeneous social backgrounds and intellectual levels than it had been for the pilot study subjects.

The present study sample was subdivided with the cutting point set at 6. While the Index was particularly effective in singling out failing readers among children from relatively higher socioeconomic backgrounds (with a minimum of False Positives), the general trend in the subgroups was toward both a high proportion of failing readers correctly identified and a high proportion of children inaccurately picked up as potential failures. The percentage of True Positives in the various subgroups ranged from 57 to 100; it was above 75 for most. False Positive rates ranged from 17 to 58 percent, falling below 40 percent in most cases.

THE MATCHED SUBSAMPLE

When a cutting point of 3 was used, the Predictive Index picked up only ten of the twenty-one failing readers in the matched subsample of the present study. When the cutting point was moved to 5, the Index identified fifteen of the twenty-one (71 percent). The Index picked up eight of the thirty-three (24 percent) who were reading adequately.

Thus, when the cutting point was shifted, the Predictive Index did identify nearly three-quarters of the failing readers in the matched subsample of the present project.

THE CALIFORNIA STUDY SAMPLE

Given a cutoff score of 3, as in the pilot study, the Predictive Index identified four of the five failing readers and picked up only six of the thirty-two children who passed. The findings in this case are quite similar to those of the original research. Therefore, in this third follow-up sample, the Predictive Index was judged to be as effective as it had been for children in the pilot study.

SUMMARY OF FINDINGS

Follow-up of the original Predictive Index showed that when used with a heterogeneous group of 282 children, the Index identified 77 percent of the failing readers and was equally effective for various subgroups. To achieve high identification levels, however, the Index cutting score had to be adjusted upward; as a result the proportion of False Positives rose to an undesirably high level.

When the early Index was used with a subsample of present study subjects matched to pilot study children by race, sex, and intelligence, it performed satisfactorily after the cutting point had been moved from 3 to 5.

The Predictive Index was judged to be as effective with the independent sample of California children as it had been for the children in the pilot study.

Discussion

Several tentative explanations are offered for the finding that the Predictive Index was less efficient when used with the large heterogeneous group than when administered to the pilot study children.

Differences in outcome are undoubtedly related to certain differences between the early study subjects and the children in the current sample. Differences between groups in IQ range may have contributed. The Index was much less efficient with the total present sample, in which IQ range was unrestricted, than for a matched subsample whose IQs were limited to a range similar to that in the early investigation. In other words, the Predictive Index worked best with children whose verbal IQs cluster around the mean.

Furthermore, socioeconomic status levels of the nonwhite children were lower in the present sample than in the pilot study. Subgroup analysis revealed that it was for just this group that the original Predictive Index was inefficient, which may have contributed to the difference in outcome.

Finally, the results demonstrated the impracticality of using the same cutoff point for widely divergent groups. While the cutting score of 3 was appropriate for the California group, it was necessary to move this score to 5 for the matched subsample, and to 6 for the large heterogeneous group, to achieve satisfactory prediction. Whatever the reason for variability in norms, it is quite clear that the cutting point must be flexible.

In summary, the follow-up study showed that the Predictive Index worked best when it was used with children who were very similar to those in the sample that served as basis for developing the early battery: It worked best with urban children of near-average intelligence who came from blue-collar homes.

What can be learned from the follow-up study? The confidence in the Predictive Index *tests* was justified. On the other hand, concern about the *norms* proved to be well founded. Because the performance of the new, heterogeneous group of children was better than that of their predecessors, the old cutoff points were of limited usefulness. (The California sample was an exception.)

It was in large measure the findings of the follow-up research that convinced the author, first, of the need for cutting scores that could be adapted to the characteristics of specific schools, and second, of the necessity to predict from a broader base, that is, to combine objective with subjective information.

Socioeconomic Rating System

Socioeconomic Status Index

Number of Points[1]	Occupation	Categories Education	Total Family Income
1	Professional Proprietor Business official Technician	At least some college	$10,000, or more
2	Salesman Clerical worker	High school graduate, or equivalent	$7,000 to 9,999
3	Skilled operator Machine operator	Some high school (Grades 9, 10, or 11)	$5,000 to 6,999
4	Service worker Unskilled manual Unemployed	Grade 8, or less	Less than $5,000

1. The index score was computed as follows: Every family received the appropriate point score for each category, and these scores were totaled. For example, a tool machine operator who was a high school graduate and who earned $9,500 per year would be rated 7. A low SES Index score represents *high* SES status, and a high SES score represents *low* SES status.

Brief Description of Second-Grade Tests

1. *Roswell-Chall Auditory Blending Test.* Children's blending performance was assessed as at kindergarten level.

2. *Bryant Phonics Test.* Ten items from the total battery were selected. Children were asked to read the printed nonsense words which embodied vowels and consonant combinations frequently encountered both in specific phonics teaching and in reading materials designed for early elementary years.

3. *Gates Advanced Primary, 1958, or Gates-MacGinitie Paragraph Reading Test, Primary B, 1965.* One or the other of these silent reading tests was administered to each child according to directions in the manuals. Scores were reduced to single digits based on equal grade score intervals.

4. *Gray Oral Reading Test, 1955 or 1967 form.* The old or the new form of this test was administered according to instructions in the manual. Scores were reduced to single digits based on equal grade score intervals.

5. *Fluency of Oral Reading (number of words per second read correctly).* One measure of the child's fluency in reading aloud was the rate per second at which he read *correctly* words in the first paragraph of the old form of the Gray Oral Test.

6. *Guessing at Words from Context.* Each child was asked to read a list of six familiar words ("cough," for example) whose graphic and phonemic patterns diverged sharply. He was then provided with sentences in which the various key words were strongly implied by context. The more fluent readers read these sentences aloud. The material was read to children who could not manage. All subjects were asked

to guess at the key word in each sentence.

7. *Written Spelling Test (Metropolitan, Grade II).* The test was administered according to specifications set out in the manual. Scores were reduced to single digits based on equal grade score intervals.

8. *Oral Spelling Test (Stanford, Grades I and II).* The subjects were asked to spell aloud fifteen words.

9. *Number of Letters Transposed (Metropolitan).* The number of times the child transposed letters in words from the Metropolitan Spelling Test was the child's score for this measure.

10. *Number of Letters Reversed (Metropolitan).* Number of letter reversals or inversions in writing the Metropolitan Spelling Test words was tallied.

11. *Number of Words in Written Composition.* The children were asked to write compositions about a cartoon sequence. The number of words used was the measure of composition length.

12. *Percentage of Correctly Spelled Words in Composition.* Of the total number of words in the written composition, the proportion spelled correctly was tabulated to get some idea of the child's ability to spell correctly in context.

Additional Tables

Table 1. Descriptive Statistics: Kindergarten Tests in Stepwise Regression Analysis (N=347)

Tests	Range (Converted Scores)	Means	Standard Deviations	Reliability
Pencil Use	1–4	1.53	.93	.32[2]
Name Writing	1–4	1.66	.96	.81[2]
Bend Gestalt	1–5	2.12	1.06	.23[3]
M Percepto Diagnostic	1–5	3.16	1.12	.77[3]
Tapped Patterns	1–5	3.08	1.25	.61[3]
Sentence Memory	1–4	1.89	.74	.40[3]
Wep Aud Discrim	1–5	2.10	1.14	
Bos Aud Discrim	1–5	2.23[1]	1.21	.80[3]
Blending	1–5	4.00[1]	1.11	.71[3]
Oral Language	1–3	1.87	.63	.65[4]
Number of Words	1–5	3.61	1.06	
Number of Diff Words	1–5	3.49	1.15	.51[5]
Categories	1–5	2.38	1.24	.55[3]
Picture Naming	1–5	3.13	1.07	.86[3]
Letter Naming	1–5	2.90	1.42	.89[3]
Horst Word Matching	1–5	2.25	1.36	.87[3]
Gates Word Matching	1–5	2.71	1.32	.52[2]
Configuration 1	1–5	3.56	1.41	.29[2]
Configuration 2	1–5	3.40	1.08	.60[2]
Word Recognition	1–3	1.48	.68	
Spelling	1–5	3.02	.99	

1. Not included in regression analysis (N=246).
2. Test-Retest (N=100).
3. Kuder-Richardson, Formula 20 (N=508).
4. Agreement between judges (N=508).
5. Parallel Form (N=52).

Table 2. Pearsonian Coefficients of Correlation Between Kindergarten Tests and Grade II Achievement Tests (N=347)

Tests	Reading	Spelling
Pencil Use	.20	.31
Name Writing	.41	.51
Bender Gestalt	.41	.44
M Percepto Diagnostic	.29	.27
Tapped Patterns	.36	.38
Sentence Memory	.36	.33
Wep Auditory Discrim	.36	.33
Bos Auditory Discrim	.42	.44
Blending	.32	.31
Oral Language	.33	.28
Number of Words	.13	.12
Number of Diff Words	.22	.21
Categories	.45	.42
Picture Naming	.54	.47
Letter Naming	.54	.60
Horst Nonsense Word Matching	.43	.42
Gates Word Matching	.45	.42
Configuration 1	.25	.23
Configuration 2	.35	.36
Word Recognition	.31	.35
Spelling	.37	.38

Table 3. Effectiveness of Screening Indexes A and B for Black and for White Boys and Girls

Variable	Percent True Positives	Percent False Positives	Percent Reading Failure
Black boys	76 (32/42)	24 (6/25)	63 (42/67)
Black girls	77 (23/30)	23 (10/44)	41 (30/74)
White boys	83 (20/24)	22 (18/81)	23 (24/105)
White girls	79 (11/14)	32 (23/73)	16 (14/87)

Table 4. Summary: Effectiveness of Screening Index for Socioeconomic Status, Age, Intelligence, and Teacher Competence Subgroups[1]

Subgroups	Black and Puerto Rican Boys and Girls and White Boys			White Girls		
	Percent True Positives	Percent False Positives	Percent Failing Readers	Percent True Positives	Percent False Positives	Percent Failing Readers
As a group	78 (81/104)	17 (27/156)	40 (104/258)	79 (11/14)	32 (23/73)	16 (14/87)
SES						
High-Middle	81 (51/63)	13 (14/119)	35 (63/182)	82 (9/11)	28 (15/54)	17 (11/65)
Low	76 (25/33)	43 (6/14)	70 (33/47)	(0/0)	(3/4)	(0/4)
Age						
Older(≥ 70 mo)	73 (37/51)	16 (16/99)	39 (51/150)	(2/4)	42 (15/36)	10 (4/40)
Ynger(≤ 69 mo)	83 (44/53)	20 (11/55)	49 (53/108)	90 (9/10)	22 (8/37)	21 (10/47)
Similarities						
High(≥ 10)	69 (22/32)	20 (11/54)	37 (32/86)	(6/7)	27 (7/26)	22 (7/33)
Low(≤ 9)	80 (8/10)	(0/3)	77 (10/13)	(1/1)	(2/3)	(1/4)
Teacher Comp						
High	87 (28/32)	15 (13/84)	28 (32/116)	(7/7)	25 (11/44)	14 (7/51)
Low	88 (37/42)	21 (6/28)	60 (42/70)	(2/4)	42 (8/19)	17 (4/23)

1. Based on a slightly different selection of children from that used in the regression analysis.

Table 5. Relationship Between Age, Socioeconomic Status, Intelligence, and Teacher Competence and Second-Grade Silent Reading Achievement

Background Variable	Coefficient of Correlation with Silent Reading Achievement	
Chronological age	(N=347)	.14
Socioeconomic status	(N=283)	.49
WISC Similarities	(N=133)	.53
Teacher competence	(N=318)	.24

Table 6. Relationship Between Predicted and Actual Reading Achievement Scores of Children Tested by Professionals and Nonprofessionals

Kindergarten Examiners	Coefficient of Correlation with Silent Reading Achievement	
Professionals		
"0"	(N=47)	.75
"2"	(N=46)	.67
"3"	(N=34)	.71
"4"	(N=16)	.78
"5"	(N= 9)	.89
Nonprofessionals		
"1"	(N=47)	.77
"6"	(N=39)	.82

The Screening Index

Instructions for Scoring

To calculate a child's score:[1]

1. For each test, mark the child's score in the appropriate place on the Score Form.

2. Turn to the appropriate score-conversion table.

3. Determine the converted score equivalent for each test score.

4. Enter converted scores on the Score Form.

5. Add converted scores.

Screening Index Score Form[2]

Test	Raw Score	Converted Score
Letter Naming	_____	_____
Picture Naming	_____	_____
Gates Word Matching	_____	_____
Bender Motor Gestalt	_____	_____
Binet Sentence Memory	_____	_____
Total	_____	

1. The calculation of a child's predicted score as based on a regression equation involves multiplying the various predictive test scores by weights, adding the products, and adding a constant.

In order to simplify this procedure, two of these steps have been done in advance for the prospective user. Specifically, weighted scores for all possible predictive test scores, corrected for the constant, have been computed. (The resulting scores are not percentile scores.) All that remains for the user to do is to convert raw scores according to the procedures described and then to add these converted scores. The score-conversion procedures have included the adjustment of data for race and sex subgroups. See pp. 156–157.

2. The tests are listed in order of their contribution to second-grade reading comprehension (not in the order in which they are to be administered).

150

Instructions for Administering the Screening Index

1. Bender Motor Gestalt Test

Material:	Cards A, 1, 2, 4, 6, 8 of the Bender Test; unlined paper; pencil.
Directions:	*Here are some designs for you to copy. Just copy them the way you see them.*
Note:	The child should be discouraged from turning the designs, but do not insist. Erasing is not permitted, but the child may cross out a design and attempt it again elsewhere on the page.

Score Criteria: Score Pass or Fail

Design A: The two figures should be in close approximation if not actual contact. One shape should be circular and the other angular.   _____

1.   The row of dots should convey linearity (random dotting is scored "fail").   _____

2.   At least two rows of dots should be shown. The rows should appear to belong to the same design. They should be quite separate from the row of dots in #1.   _____

4.   The two figures should be shown as related parts but need not touch. One shape should be curving, the other angular; both designs should be open on one side.   _____

6.   The lines should cross at or near the center, but they need not be wavy.   _____

8.   The figure should be elongated though not necessarily angular. The inner figure should be centered; it should be more than a straight line.   _____

Score: From 0 to 6; the number of copies rated
                as passing.

                            Score:
                            Bender   _____

2. Gates Word Matching Test

Material: Word Matching Subtest from Gates
                Reading Readiness Battery; a pencil; a
                shield.

Note: Proceeding left to right, child is to at-
                tempt exercises 2, 3, 4, 5, 8, 9, 10, 11, 14,
                15, 16, and 17.

                Examiner shields all but the first exer-
                cise, saying,

Directions: *There are two words in this box which*
                look exactly alike. Can you find them?
                Take your pencil and draw a line be-
                tween the ones that look the same. . . .
                Now, you do the next one by yourself.

                If the child fails to understand what is
                required, the examiner may clarify it, us-
                ing the first exercise as an example, in
                any way that seems appropriate. The
                shield is removed after exercises 2 and
                3.

Score: From 0 to 12; the number of word-pairs
                correctly matched.

                            Score:
                Gates Word Matching   _____

3. Letter Naming

Material: Six index cards on which letters are
                printed in capitals with black ink.

Directions: *What letter is this? And this?*
                A_____F_____K_____J_____C_____B
                (check letters correctly named)
                (note mistakes)

Score: From 0 to 6; the number of letters cor-
            rectly named.

Score:
Letter Naming   _____

4. Picture Naming

Material: Notebook containing 22 line drawings;
                answer form.

Directions: *I want to see how many pictures you can
                name. What do you call this?*

Note: Record child's responses on answer
                form.

Score: From 0 to 22; the number of pictures
                child named correctly on *very first utter-
                ance.*

Score:
Picture Naming   _____

Picture Names

	Scored "Correct"	Very First Response	Credit
1.	hot dog, frank, frankfurter, wiener	_____	____
2.	kite	_____	____
3.	nest, bird nest, eggs	_____	____
4.	badge, medal, pin	_____	____
5.	letter, envelope, mail, postcard, card	_____	____
6.	whale	_____	____
7.	queen, princess (must ident. as *woman*); king, prince (must ident. as *man*)	_____	____
8.	window	_____	____
9.	shovel, spade	_____	____
10.	dial	_____	____
11.	dentist (Ex. points to d.)	_____	____
12.	slingshot	_____	____
13.	fireplace	_____	____

14.	parachute (Ex. points to chute)	_____	___
15.	kangaroo	_____	___
16.	vegetables, food, salad, greens (Ex. says: *These are all* . . .)	_____	___
17.	mountain	_____	___
18.	chimney (Ex. points to ch.)	_____	___
19.	binoculars, field glasses	_____	___
20.	projector	_____	___
21.	veterinarian, vet	_____	___
22.	scientist, chemist	_____	___

Total number of pictures named correctly ___

5. Binet Sentence Memory[1]

Material: List of sentences examiner is to read to the child.

Note: The child must repeat each sentence EXACTLY as spoken by examiner. When the child repeats correctly one sentence at a level, go on to next level, skipping the alternative. Do not repeat sentence when child makes an error, but ask child to repeat alternate sentence at same level. If he fails the second sentence at any level, continue for one more level. He discontinues, thus, either because he has repeated a sentence at every level correctly or because he has failed *both* sentences at *two consecutive* levels.

Directions: *Can you say "big boy"? (or "big girl")* . . . *Good. Can you say, "I am a big boy"?* (or *"big girl"*) *Now, can you say:*

Pass or Fail

Age 4:   I like to eat ice-cream cones.   _____
              My watch has two hands.   _____
              Give me just one of them.   _____

1. Binet test items are provided with permission of Houghton Mifflin Company, Boston.

Age 5:   Jane wants to put a big table in her play-
                house.[2]   _____
                Tom has lots of fun playing ball with his
                sister.   _____

Age 7:   Betty has made a pretty dress for her
                doll out of blue ribbon.   _____
                My baby brother wants Santa Claus to
                bring him a great big drum.   _____

Score: From 0 to 3; the number of age levels at
                which the child repeated sentences cor-
                rectly.

                              Score:
                              Binet Sentence
                              Memory   _____

2. The sentence shown was substituted for the corresponding Binet item.

Table 1. Converted Scores for Black Boys

Letter Naming		Picture Naming		Gates Matching		Bender		Sentence Memory	
RS[1]	CS[2]	RS	CS	RS	CS	RS	CS	RS	CS
0	0	0	−3	0	−1	0	−1	0	0
1	6	1	−2	1	−1	1	1	1	6
2	10	2	−1	2	0	2	3	2	12
3	11	3	1	3	1	3	5	3	18
4	13	4	2	4	1	4	9		
5	17	5	3	5	3	5	13		
6	23	6	4	6	5	6	17		
		7	6	7	6				
		8	8	8	8				
		9	9	9	10				
		10	11	10	12				
		11	13	11	14				
		12	14	12	16				
		13	16						
		14	18						
		15	19						
		16	21						
		17	23						
		18	24						
		19	25						
		20	27						
		21	28						
		22	29						

1. Raw score (RS) is number of correct responses.
2. Converted score (CS).

Table 2. Converted Scores for Black Girls

Letter Naming		Picture Naming		Gates Matching		Bender		Sentence Memory	
RS[1]	CS[2]	RS	CS	RS	CS	RS	CS	RS	CS
0	0	0	−3	0	−2	0	−1	0	0
1	6	1	−2	1	−1	1	1	1	6
2	10	2	−1	2	0	2	4	2	13
3	13	3	1	3	1	3	6	3	19
4	15	4	2	4	2	4	10		
5	19	5	3	5	3	5	14		
6	25	6	5	6	5	6	19		
		7	6	7	7				
		8	8	8	9				
		9	10	9	11				
		10	12	10	13				
		11	14	11	15				
		12	16	12	17				
		13	17						
		14	19						
		15	21						
		16	23						
		17	25						
		18	26						
		19	28						
		20	29						
		21	31						
		22	32						

1. Raw score (RS) is number of correct responses.
2. Converted score (CS).

Table 3. Converted Scores for White Boys

Letter Naming		Picture Naming		Gates Matching		Bender		Sentence Memory	
RS[1]	CS[2]	RS	CS	RS	CS	RS	CS	RS	CS
0	0	0	−2	0	−1	0	−1	0	0
1	5	1	−1	1	−1	1	1	1	5
2	8	2	0	2	0	2	3	2	10
3	10	3	0	3	1	3	5	3	15
4	11	4	1	4	1	4	7		
5	14	5	2	5	2	5	11		
6	19	6	4	6	4	6	15		
		7	5	7	5				
		8	6	8	7				
		9	8	9	8				
		10	9	10	10				
		11	11	11	12				
		12	12	12	13				
		13	13						
		14	15						
		15	16						
		16	18						
		17	19						
		18	20						
		19	21						
		20	23						
		21	24						
		22	25						

1. Raw score (RS) is number of correct responses.
2. Converted score (CS).

Table 4. Converted Scores for White Girls

Letter Naming		Picture Naming		Gates Matching		Bender		Sentence Memory	
RS[1]	CS[2]	RS	CS	RS	CS	RS	CS	RS	CS
0	0	0	−2	0	−1	0	−1	0	0
1	4	1	−1	1	−1	1	1	1	5
2	7	2	0	2	0	2	3	2	9
3	9	3	0	3	1	3	4	3	14
4	10	4	1	4	1	4	7		
5	13	5	2	5	2	5	10		
6	18	6	3	6	4	6	14		
		7	5	7	5				
		8	6	8	6				
		9	7	9	8				
		10	8	10	9				
		11	10	11	11				
		12	11	12	12				
		13	12						
		14	14						
		15	15						
		16	16						
		17	18						
		18	19						
		19	20						
		20	21						
		21	22						
		22	23						

1. Raw score (RS) is number of correct responses.
2. Converted score (CS).

The Diagnostic Battery

The Diagnostic Test Battery is to be administered to kindergarten children identified by the Screening Index as being at risk of failing. Diagnostic test results provide a profile of a child's weakness and strength in competences that were shown to be relevant for reading. This information should be useful for educational planning.

The Diagnostic Test Battery is divided into two sections. Part I includes tests and ratings that were experimentally derived. The tests selected were those that best characterized their respective factors, and the factors represented in the battery are those that were most closely related to reading. The Part II items, which were suggested by clinical experience, are behaviors to be judged by the teacher.

Part I measures for which scores are to be obtained are:
Name Writing
Nonsense Word Matching
Blending
Speech Sound Discrimination
Tapped Patterns
Category Names
Oral Language Level
Word Recognition
Spelling Two Words Previously Taught
Pencil Use
Question: What Is Reading?[1]

1. This item was not experimentally derived. It was listed in Part I for administrative convenience.

It is recommended that the tests be administered in the order shown in Part I so as to keep the children's interest and attention at as high a level as possible. The scores for the measures should be entered on the Diagnostic Test Battery form.

The children will already have scores for the five previously administered tests obtained during the *predictive* screening phase. The scores of all five are to be transferred to appropriate listings in the Diagnostic Test Battery form.

The tests administered during the predictive screening phase were those that made up the Screening Index. To review, these tests were:

Letter Naming
Picture Naming
Gates Word Matching
Bender Motor Gestalt
Binet Sentence Memory

When "new" and "old" scores have been recorded, the examiner refers to the Rating sheet, which characterizes scores for each test as "Good," "Fair," or "Poor." When the ratings for all of the measures have been determined, they are ranked under each factor according to the extent of their contribution to the factor.

The seven items that make up *Part II* of the Diagnostic Test Battery should be rated by the teacher. Once these ratings have been made, these too are transferred to the Diagnostic Profile form.

A glance at the completed Diagnostic Profile gives an impression of the child's abilities and behaviors that are important for reading. Occasionally the rating of tests that reflect a given factor do not produce a consistent picture. For example, ratings might be "Good" on some and "Fair" or "Poor" on other tests in the same category. In appraising the child's status on the ability in question, one should give most weight to the top-ranked test because it contributes the most.

The procedures for administering and scoring the Diagnostic Test Battery may be summarized as follows:

1. Administer and score the measures listed in Part I.
2. Determine "Good"-"Fair"-"Poor" characterizations for scores on Part I tests by referring to the Rating form (p. 171).
3. Arrange for the teacher to evaluate behaviors itemized in Part II.
4. Transfer Part I and Part II ratings to the Diagnostic Profile sheet.

Diagnostic Test Battery

Part I. Tests that Reflect the Four Factors: Oral Language A, Pattern Matching, Pattern Memory, and Visuo Motor Organization

Introduction to Tests 8 and 9:

Material:	The words "boy" and "train" printed in black ink on two index cards; ruled paper; pencil.
Directions:	*I am going to teach you how to read two words.* (Examiner exposes the word "boy.") *This word is "boy," like "you are a boy."* (Or, like "a boy in your class.") *Now, you say it. That's right, you can read "boy." Now here is another word: "train." See, it is long, just as a train is long. This word is "train." Now you read "train."* (Examiner takes up both index cards and holds them, one behind the other, "boy" in front.) *Now this is "boy," remember, and* (exposes "train") *this is "train." Now let's see if you can read them by yourself.* (Shows "boy.") *What does this say? Right, it says "boy."* (Shows "train.") *And what does this say? Right, it says "train."* (Examiner then places cards side by side on the table.) *What is this word? Right, it is "boy." And what is this word? Yes, it's "train."* (The examiner repeats consecutive and side-by-side exposures one or two more times, until she is convinced that, at least for the moment, the child can "read" the words.) *Now I want you to write the words on this piece of paper. Write "boy" first. Good. Now write "train" here. Remember that this is "boy"* (shows child the word) *and this is "train"* (shows "train"). (This completes introduction phase. A review will follow Test 5, and the word-recognition and spelling tasks are Test 8 and 9.)

1. Name Writing (first name only)

Material:	Unlined paper; pencil.
Directions:	*Write your name on this paper.*
Rating:	0—spells 0 letters of name.
	1—spells 1 letter of name.

2—spells more than one letter, but spelling is incorrect.

3—spells first name correctly.

Score: From 0 to 3, according to above criteria.

> Score:
> Name Writing_____

2. Nonsense Word Matching Test[2]

Material: Nonsense Word Matching Test form; pencil.

Directions: *Look at all of these along here.* (Examiner indicates the nonsense words in the top row, which is the practice row. He points to the key pattern, the one to be matched, which is at the left of the top row.) *Tell me which one of these others looks exactly like the one I have my finger on.* (If child indicates a reverse pattern, examiner shows him a correct one and says:) *No, look here. This is like the one by my finger. See, it starts with a circle and ends with a sort of cane. Draw a line through it. Now, can you find another one that looks the same? Do this row by yourself. Draw a line through all the ones that are like the one by my finger.*

Note: All but the practice row are shielded. When child understands task, examiner directs him to row 2, as above. After child completes row 2, shield is removed. The examiner may help child by pointing to the configurations to be compared. However, child is encouraged to take over the task himself.

Score: From 0 to 9, the number of rows in which child has identified all correct matches.

> Score:
> Nonsense Word Matching_____

3. Roswell-Chall Auditory Blending Test (partial)[3]

Directions: *I am going to divide words into parts and I want you to put them together again. Listen, what word am I saying: "n-ose"?* (Ex. touches own nose.) *That's right, I said "nose." Now, what word is this: "t-op"?*

2. This test was substituted for the Horst and is quite similar to it in format.
3. Permission granted by Essay Press, Inc. for reprinting.

Yes, it's "top." And what word is this: "s-i-t"? Yes, I said "sit." Now let's try these others:

Words to
Blend:

a. n-o ____   e. f-at ____   h. t-ime ____
b. u-p ____   f. pl-ay ____   i. c-a-t ____
c. s-ay ____   g. c-ake ____   j. b-i-g ____
d. m-y ____

Score:
From 0 to 10, the number of words correctly blended.

Score:
Blending____

4. Boston Speech Sound Discrimination Test

Material:
Folder showing line drawings of pairs of pictures; these represent words that are spoken so that twelve of the pairs contrast phonemically. On each of thirteen pages, a pair of pictures is shown three times.

Directions:
Let's look at these pictures. (Examiner opens to page of sample items.) *Point to the pictures I name: "cat —cat." That's right. Here is "cat—cat." Now point to "cat—bat." Good. Now let's try some more.*

Note:
When convinced child understands, examiner continues with the test itself.

Words to Be
Compared:

a. pin-pin ____   m. pen-pin ____
b. cone-comb ____   n. cone-cone ____
c. clown-crown ____   o. crown-crown ____
d. pen-pen ____   p. pan-pen ____
e. lock-lock ____   q. log-lock ____
f. rock-rock ____   r. rock-lock ____
g. wash-wash ____   s. wash-watch ____
h. face-face ____   t. vase-face ____
i. mouse-mouth ____   u. mouth-mouth ____
j. knot-nut ____   v. knot-knot ____
k. cat-cat ____   w. cap-cat ____
l. three-three ____   x. tree-three ____

Score:
From 0 to 24, the number of correct discriminations.

Score:
Sound Discrimination____

5. Tapped Patterns

Material:	One mallet; cardboard shield.
Directions:	*I will tap and you make it sound the way mine does: / / That's right. There were two loud taps. Now let's do two soft ones: . . You do it now. Good! Now try this: . / One was soft, the other loud. You do it. Now let's do some more.*
Note:	The examiner taps out the patterns behind a shield, then hands mallet to child. There should be about 1/2 second between taps.

Score Pass or Fail

Patterns:	/ .	_____
	. . /	_____
	/ . . /	_____
	/ . / . /	_____
	/ / . . / /	_____

Score:	From 0 to 5, the number of patterns tapped out correctly.

Score:
Tapped Patterns_____

•Review for Tests 8 and 9, Word Recognition and Spelling Two Words Previously Taught ("boy" and "train"):

Note:	Review the words "boy" and "train" with the child, as described on page 162. Child should not, however, copy words a second time.

6. Category Names

Directions:	*What are these things: Tom—Charley—Henry?* (If the child does not respond by saying "boys," "names," "people," "men," or "brothers," continue:) *I'll tell you about three other things: ball—doll—marbles. They are all toys. Now tell me, what are Tom—Charley—Henry?*

Pass or Fail

Categories and Correct Responses:	Tom—Charley—Henry (boys, names, people, men, brothers)	_____

red—green—blue   (colors)   _____
apple—hamburger—   (food, lunch,
ice cream   supper, meal) _____
saw—hammer—   (tools)
screwdriver   _____

Score: From 0 to 4, the number of categories correctly named.

Score:
Category Names_____

7. Oral Language Level

Material: Tape recorder; two cartoon sequences: "Fire" and "Fish."

Note: Sequences are set out before the child. Tape recorder should be turned on just before he begins. Start with "Fire."

Directions: *You see, these pictures make a story. You tell it. Start here.* (If child hesitates:) *Just tell me in your own words what is happening in the pictures.* (After he finishes first story:) *That was fine. Now here is another. Tell me about this one.*

Note: After child is tested, the examiner listens to the tape-recorded stories. Ratings are based on the child's ability to organize the material (to sequence events and to tell the point of the story), on syntactical maturity, and on freedom from articulatory errors. Colloquialisms and variations in dialect are *not* considered errors.

Rating: 0—difficulty with grammar, or with articulation, or with organization of the story rendering story unintelligible.

1—difficulty with one or more of above three is present but does not prevent child from communicating a story with a conclusion.

2—story well organized; grammar mature; articulation at level expected of age.

Score: From 0 to 2, according to rating.

Score:
Oral Language Level_____

8. Word Recognition

Material:	Words "boy" and "train" and eight additional words written on index cards.

Note: The words are arranged on the table as follows:

dog	fame	boy	
yet	snail	man	
train	lake	drone	great

Directions: *You remember the two words you learned at the beginning today? They were "boy" and "train." I have put them here on the table along with some other words you don't know. I want you to see if you can find the words "boy" then "train." Be sure to look at all of the words.*

(Examiner encourages child to look at all the words and tries to prevent him from choosing too hastily.)

Rating:
0—finds neither "boy" nor "train."
1—finds either, but not both.
2—finds both "boy" and "train."

Score: From 0 to 2, according to above criteria.

Score:
Word Recognition_____

9. Spelling of Two Words Previously Taught

Material: Words "boy" and "train" printed in black ink on two index cards; ruled paper; pencil.

Note: After child has made his choices as required for #8, the examiner takes cards from the table. She exposes "boy" and "train" briefly, then puts both out of sight.

Directions: *Write the words "boy" and "train" on this paper.*

Rating: Number of points:

"boy"		"train"	
3—word spelled correctly	_____	3—word spelled correctly	_____
2—two or three letters written, ten regardless of order	_____	2—three, four, or five letters regardless of order	_____
1—one letter written	_____	1—one or two letters	_____

0—failure to   0—failure to
  recall any   recall any
  letters   _____   letters   _____

Score: From 0 to 6, total of points for correct spelling (total for "boy" total for "train").

Score:
Spelling_____

10. Pencil Use

Note: The child is observed throughout the evaluation as he uses the pencil.

Rating: 0—shows such severe difficulties with pencil management that he either tears the paper or marks so faintly that the result is scarcely visible.

1—has considerable difficulty with pencil management.

2—has some trouble with management.

3—uses pencil proficiently.

Score: From 0 to 3, according to rating.

Score:
Pencil Use_____

Summary of Scores on Tests of the Predictive Screening Index:

1. Letter Naming

Score: From 0 to 6, the number of letters correctly named.

Score:
Letter Naming_____

2. Picture Naming

Score: From 0 to 22, the number of pictures correctly named on very first response.

Score:
Picture Naming _____

3. Gates Word Matching

Score: From 0 to 12, the number of correct matches.

Score:
Gates Word Matching_____

4. Bender Motor Gestalt

    Score: From 0 to 6, the number of copies rated as passing.

                                  Score:
                                  Bender Motor Gestalt_____

5. Binet Sentence Memory

    Score: From 0 to 3, the number of age levels at which sentences are repeated correctly.

                                  Score:
                                  Binet Sentence
                                  Memory_____

An Additional Question—Understanding of What Reading Is:

    Adult: *What is reading?* or *What do we mean when we say "reading"?*
    Child: Reading is _____

    Rating:
        Poor—   says "don't know" or otherwise fails to cope with question.
        Fair—   associates descriptively to word "reading," that is, "reading a book," or "reading a story."
        Good—   refers in some manner to the correspondence between written and spoken words.

Part II. Additional Observations and Impressions

1. Ability to Listen

    Rating:
        Poor—   disinterested, wanders around room or plays when teacher is telling story; cannot answer questions about the story.
        Fair—   listening and comprehension vary; although child may understand the gist of the story, he often misses the fine points.
        Good—   listens well, interested; full comprehension, including grasp of relationship between details and whole.

2. Understanding of Directions

Rating:
Poor—   frequently misunderstands; often asks for repetition; trouble remembering more than one command.
Fair—   occasional misunderstanding; can cope with two or three simple commands at once, but may confuse sequence or details.
Good—   usually follows directions correctly; can cope with several complicated directions.

3. Need to Move About

Rating:
Poor—   constantly moves in seat; falls off chair frequently; gets up if adult leaves him.
Fair—   can sit for a short period; may move about quite a bit in chair, or may slump, or alternate between the two.
Good—   can sit quietly for long periods.

4. Pleasure in Working with Crayons and Pencil

Rating:
Poor—   rarely selects graphomotor activity.
Fair—   selects and enjoys occasionally; needs to be urged.
Good—   frequently elects such activities; expresses pleasure in drawing or writing.

5. Working Alone

Rating:
Poor—   needs constant guidance.
Fair—   can work alone up to a point but works much less well than when he has guidance.
Good—   can take over task himself.

6. Persistence

Rating:
Poor—   gives up immediately.
Fair—   persistence depends on success.
Good—   works well and hard from start to finish, despite obstacles along the way.

7. Independent Thinking

Rating:
Poor—   rarely or never produces an idea or observation of his own.

Fair— occasionally offers independent opinion or new suggestion.

Good— frequently offers independent opinion; makes objective judgments and sensible decisions.

Rating Diagnostic Battery Test Scores

Test	Rating		
	Poor	Fair	Good
Name Writing	0–1	2	3
Nonsense Word Matching[1]	0–4	5–8	9
Blending	0–1	2–3	4–10
Boston Sound Discrimination	0–10	11–20	21–24
Tapped Patterns	0–2	3	4–5
Category Names	0–1	2–3	4
Word Recognition	0	1	2
Spelling Two Words	0–1	2–3	4–6
Pencil Use	0–1	2	3
Oral Language	0	1	2
Letter Naming	0–1	2–5	6
Picture Naming	0–8	9–15	16–22
Gates Word Matching	0–5	6–8	9–12
Bender Motor Gestalt	0–3	4–5	6
Sentence Memory	0–1	2	3

1. Scoring criteria based on a sample of 52 children.

Diagnostic Profile

Test	Rating		
	Poor	Fair	Good

Part I. Abilities (Factors)

Oral Language A

Picture Naming

Oral Language Level

Category Names

Sentence Memory

Boston Sound Discrimination

Letter Naming

Pattern Matching

Gates Word Matching

Nonsense Word Matching

Tapped Patterns

Sentence Memory

Pattern Memory

Blending

Word Recognition

Spelling Two Words

Boston Sound Discrimination

Letter Naming

Visuo Motor Organization

Pencil Use

Bender Motor Gestalt

Name Writing

Spelling Two Words

Question: What Is Reading?

Diagnostic Profile

Test	Rating		
	Poor	Fair	Good

Part II. Additional Observations and Impressions

Ability to Listen

Understanding Directions

Need to Move About

Pleasure: Crayons and Pencil

Working Alone

Persistence

Independent Thinking

Bibliography

Introduction

Brezeinski, J. and Howard, W.   Early reading—how, not when. *Reading Teacher*, 1971, *25*, 240.

1. Approaches to Prediction

Ames, L. B., and Walker, R. N.   Prediction of later reading ability from kindergarten Rorschach and IQ scores. *Journal of Educational Psychology*, 1964, *55* (6), 309–313.

Austin, M. C., and Morrison, C.   *The First R: The Harvard Report on Reading in Elementary Schools.* New York: Macmillan, 1963.

Bagford, J.   Reading readiness scores and success in reading. *Reading Teacher*, 1968, *21*, 324–328.

Baratz, J. C., and Shuy, R. W. (Eds.).   *Teaching Black Children to Read.* Washington, D.C.: Center for Applied Linguistics, 1969.

Barrett, T. C.   The relationship between measures of pre-reading visual discrimination and first grade reading achievement: A review of the literature. *Reading Research Quarterly*, 1965a, *1* (1), 51–76.

Barrett, T. C.   Visual discrimination tasks as predictors of first grade reading achievement. *Reading Teacher*, 1965b, *18*, 276–282.

Bender, L.   *A Visual Motor Gestalt Test and Its Clinical Use.* New York: American Orthopsychiatric Association, 1938.

Bender, L.   Problems in conceptualization and communication in children with developmental alexia. In P. H. Hoch and J. Zubin (Eds.), *Psychopathology of Communication.* New York: Grune & Stratton, 1958.

175

Bender, L.   The visual motor gestalt function in six-and seven-year-old normal and schizophrenic children. In J. Zubin and G. A. Jervis (Eds.), *Psychopathology of Mental Development.* New York: Grune & Stratton, 1967.

Benton, A.   Right-left discrimination. *Pediatric Clinics of North America,* 1968, *15*, 747–758.

Berko, J.   The child's learning of English morphology. *Word,* 1958, *14*, 150–177.

Berry, M.   *Language Disorders of Children: The Bases and Diagnosis.* New York: Appleton-Century-Crofts, 1969.

Birch, H. G.   Research issues in child health: Some philosophic and methodologic issues. *Pediatrics,* 1970, *45* (5), 874–883.

Birch, H. G., and Belmont, L.   Auditory-visual integration, intelligence and reading ability in school children. *Perceptual and Motor Skills,* 1965a, *20,* 295–305.

Birch, H. G., and Belmont, L.   Social differences in auditory perception. *Perceptual and Motor Skills,* 1965b, *20,* 861–870.

Blanchard, P.   Psychoanalytic contributions to problems of reading disability. In R. S. Eissler *et al.* (Eds.), *Psychoanalytic Study of the Child.* Vol. 2. New York: International Universities Press, 1946.

Blank, M.   Cognitive processes in auditory discrimination in normal and retarded readers. *Child Development,* 1968, *39* (4), 1091–1101.

Blank, M. and Bridger, W. H.   Perceptual abilities and conceptual deficiencies in retarded readers. In J. Zubin and G. A. Jervis (Eds.), *Psychopathology of Mental Development.* New York: Grune & Stratton, 1967.

Bliesmer, E.   A study of relationships among tests of reading readiness, teachers' predictions, test intelligence and reading achievement. Unpublished M.A. thesis, State University of Iowa, 1951.

Bond, G. L. and Dykstra, R.   The cooperative research program in first grade reading instruction. *Reading Research Quarterly,* 1967, *2* (4), 5–142.

Bougere, M. B.   Selected factors in oral language related to first-grade reading achievement. *Reading Research Quarterly,* 1969, *5* (1), 31–58.

Bremer, N. D.   Do readiness tests predict success in reading? *Elementary School Journal,* 1959, *59,* 222–224.

Brown, R., and Bellugi, U.   Three processes in the child's acquisition of syntax. *Harvard Educational Review,* 1964, *34,* 133–151.

Bryan, Q.   Relative importance of intelligence and visual perception in predicting reading achievement. *California Journal of Educational Research,* 1964, *15,* 44–48.

Bryant, P. E.   Comments on the design of developmental studies of cross-modal matching and cross-modal transfer. *Cortex*, 1968, *4* (2), 127–137.

Buktenica, N. A.   Perceptual mode dominance: An approach to assessment of first-grade reading and spelling. In *Proceedings, 76th Annual Convention, American Psychological Association*. Washington, D.C.: American Psychological Association, 1968.

Cazden, C. B.   The acquisition of noun and verb inflections. *Child Development*, 1968, *39*, 433–448.

Chall, J.   *Learning to Read: The Great Debate*. New York: McGraw-Hill, 1967.

Chall, J., Roswell, F., and Blumenthal, S.   Auditory blending ability: A factor in success in beginning reading. *Reading Teacher*, 1963, *17*, 113–118.

Clymer, T.   How good is research in reading? In N. B. Smith (Ed.), *Current Issues in Reading*. International Reading Association Conference Proceedings, Vol. 13, Part 2. Newark, Del.: International Reading Association, 1969.

Coleman, J. M., Iscoe, I., and Brodsky, M.   Draw-a-man test as a predictor of school readiness and as an index of emotional and physical maturity. *Pediatrics*, 1959, *24*, 275–281.

de Hirsch, K.   Concepts related to normal reading processes and their application to reading pathology. *Journal of Genetic Psychology*, 1963, *102*, 277–285.

de Hirsch, K., and Jansky, J. J.   Early predictions of reading, writing and spelling ability. *British Journal of Communication Disorders*, 1966, *1*, 99–107.

de Hirsch, K., Jansky, J. J., and Langford, W. S.   *Predicting Reading Failure*. New York: Harper & Row, 1966.

Durkin, D.   Children who read before grade one. *Reading Teacher*, 1961, *14*, 163–166.

Durkin, D.   *Children Who Read Early*. New York: Teachers College Press, 1966.

Durrell, D. D.   First grade reading success study: A summary. *Journal of Education*, 1958, *140* (3), 1–6.

Dykstra, R.   Auditory discrimination abilities and beginning reading achievement. *Reading Research Quarterly*, 1966, *1* (3), 5–34.

Dykstra, R.   The use of reading readiness tests for diagnosis and prediction: A critique. In T. C. Barrett (Ed.), *The Evaluation of Children's Reading Achievement*. Newark, Del.: International Reading Association, 1967.

Dykstra, R.   Some thoughts about predicting achievement in reading. Unpublished paper, 1968.

Elkind, D., and Scott, L.   Studies in perceptual development: I. The decentering of perception. *Child Development*, 1962, *33*, 619–630.

Ermalinski, R., and Ruscelli, V.   Incorporation of values by lower and middle socioeconomic class preschool boys. *Child Development,* 1971, *42,* 629–632.

Escalona, S., and Heider, G.   *Prediction and Outcome: A Study of Child Development.* New York: Basic Books, 1959.

Eustis, R. S.   Specific reading disorder. *New England Journal of Medicine,* 1947, *237,* 243–249.

Feldmann, S. C.   Evaluation of pre-reading skills. In M. M. Clark and S. M. Maxwell (Eds.), *Reading: Influences on Progress.* Proceedings of the Fifth Annual Study Congress of the United Kingdom Reading Association, Edinburgh, 1967–68.

Fendric, P., and McGlade, C. A.   A validation of two prognostic tests of reading aptitude. *Elementary School Journal,* 1938, *39,* 187–194.

Fransella, F., and Gerber, D.   Multiple regression equations for predicting reading age from chronological age and WISC verbal IQ. *British Journal of Educational Psychology,* 1965, *35,* 86–89.

Freud, A.   *Normality and Pathology in Childhood.* New York: International Universities Press, 1965.

Gates, A. I.   The necessary mental age for beginning reading. *Elementary School Journal,* 1937, *37,* 497–508.

Gates, A. I., and MacGinitie, W. H.   *Gates-MacGinitie Reading Tests: Readiness Skills.* New York: Teachers College Press, 1968.

Gavel, S. R.   June reading achievements of first grade children. *Journal of Education,* 1958, *140* (3), 37–43.

Gesell, A.   *The First Five Years of Life.* New York: Harper & Row, 1940.

Gibson, E. J.   Perceptual development. In H. W. Stevenson (Ed.), *Child Psychology.* Sixty-second yearbook of the National Society for the Study of Education, Part 1. Chicago: University of Chicago Press, 1963.

Gibson, E. J., Gibson, J. J., Pick, A., and Osser, H. H.   A developmental study of discrimination of letter-like forms. *Journal of Comparative and Physiological Psychology,* 1962, *55,* 897–906.

Goffeney, B., Henderson, N. B., and Butler, B. V.   Negro-white male-female eight-month developmental scores compared with seven-year WISC and Bender test scores. *Child Development,* 1971, *42,* 595–604.

Goins, J. T.   Visual Perceptual Abilities and Early Reading Progress. Supplementary Educational Monographs No. 87. Chicago: University of Chicago Press, 1958.

Goodenough, F. L.   *Measurement of Intelligence by Drawings.* Yonkers-on-Hudson: World Book, 1926.

Goodman, K. S.   A linguistic study of cues and miscues in reading. *Elementary English,* 1965, *42,* 639–643.

Goodman, K. S.   Analysis of oral reading miscues: Applied psycholinguistics. *Reading Research Quarterly*, 1969, 5 (1), 9–30.

Gordon, E. W.   Introduction. *Review of Educational Research*, 1970, *40* (1), 1–12.

Gottesman, R. L.   Auditory discrimination ability in standard English speaking and Negro dialect speaking children. Unpublished Ph.D. thesis, Teachers College, Columbia University, 1968.

Hallgren, B.   Specific dyslexia: A clinical and genetic study. *Acta Psychiatrica and Neurologica*, 1950, Supp. 65, 1–287.

Harris, A. J.   The effective teacher of reading. *Reading Teacher*, 1969, *23*, 195–204.

Haywood, H. C.   Experimental factors in intellectual development: The concept of dynamic intelligence. In J. Zubin and G. A. Jervis (Eds.), *Psychopathology of Mental Development*. New York: Grune & Stratton, 1967.

Hermann, K., and Norrie, E.   Is congenital word blindness a hereditary type of Gerstmann's syndrome? *Psychiatrica et Neurologica*, 1958, *136*, 59–73.

Hertzig, M. E., Birch, H. G., Thomas, A., and Mendez, O. A.   *Class and Ethnic Differences in the Responsiveness of Preschool Children to Cognitive Demands*. Monograph of the Society of Research in Child Development, Serial No. 117, 1968, *33* (1).

Hess, R., and Shipman, V.   Early experiences and the socialization of cognitive modes in children. *Child Development*, 1965, *36*, 869–886.

Hildreth, G., and Griffiths, N.   *Metropolitan Readiness Tests*. New York: Harcourt, Brace & World, 1950.

Hirst, W. E.   *Identification in the Kindergarten of Factors That Make for Future Success in Reading*. Final report, Project No. OE-6-10-023. Washington, D.C.: U.S. Department of Health, Education and Welfare, 1969.

Ilg, F. L., and Ames, L. B.   *School Readiness: Behavior Tests Used at the Gesell Institute*. New York: Harper & Row, 1965.

Inizan, A.   *Le temps d'apprendre à lire*. Collection Bourrelier, Librairie Armand. Paris: Colin, 1966.

Jansky, J. J.   The contribution of certain kindergarten abilities to second grade reading and spelling achievement. Unpublished Ph.D. thesis, Columbia University, 1970.

Johansson, R. B.   *Criteria of School Readiness*. Stockholm Studies in Educational Psychology. Uppsala: Almquist & Wiksell, 1965.

Johnson, D.   Paper read at the Annual Meeting of the Orton Society, Boston, 1971.

Johnson, R. E.   The validity of the Clymer-Barrett Pre-reading Battery. *Reading Teacher*, 1969, *22*, 609–614.

Kagan, J.   Continuity in cognitive development during the first year. *Merrill-Palmer Quarterly*, 1969, *15*, 101–120.

Kainz, F.   *Psychologie der Sprache*. Stuttgart: Ferdinand Enke Verlag, 1956.

Karlin, R.   The prediction of reading success and reading readiness tests. *Elementary English*, 1957, *34*, 320–322.

Kawi, A. A., and Pasamanick, B.   Association of factors of pregnancy and reading disorders in childhood. *Journal of the American Medical Association*, 1958, *166*, 1420–1423.

Kimura, D.   Cerebral dominance and the perception of verbal stimuli. *Canadian Journal of Psychology*, 1961, *15*, 166–171.

Kingston, A. J.   The relationship of first grade readiness to third and fourth grade achievement. *Journal of Educational Research*, 1962, *56* (2), 61–67.

Kolers, P. A.   Reading is only incidentally visual. In K. Goodman and J. Fleming (Eds.), *Psycholinguistics and the Teaching of Reading*. Newark, Del.: International Reading Association, 1969.

Koppitz, E., Mardis, V., and Stephens, T. S.   A note on screening school beginners with the Bender gestalt test. *Journal of Educational Psychology*, 1961, *52* (2), 80–81.

Labov, W., Cohen, P., Robbins, C., and Lewis, J.   *A Study of the Nonstandard English of Negro and Puerto Rican Speakers in New York City*. Washington, D.C.: U.S. Office of Education, Department of Health, Education and Welfare, 1968.

Lambert, N.   Predicting and evaluating the effectiveness of children in school. In E. M. Bower and W. G. Hollister (Eds.), *Behavioral Science Frontiers in Education*. New York: Wiley, 1967.

Lauderville, Sister M. F.   A study of the effectiveness of a first-grade listening test as a predictor of reading achievement. Unpublished doctoral dissertation, State University of Iowa, 1958.

Lee, J. M., and Clark, W.   *Lee-Clark Reading Readiness Test. Revised*. Monterey, Calif.: California Test Bureau, 1962.

Lee, L. L.   *Northwestern Syntax Screening Test*. Evanston, Ill.: Northwestern University Press, 1969.

Liberman, I. Y.   Speech and lateralization of language. *Bulletin of the Orton Society*, 1971, *21*, 71–86.

Lindemann, E., Allinsmith, W., Rosenblith, J. F., Budd, L. M., and Shapiro, S.   Evaluation of a pre-school screening program. *American Journal of Orthopsychiatry*, 1963, *33*, 376–377.

Lowell, R.   Selected reading readiness tests as predictors of success in reading. U.S. Office of Education Project No. 6-8894. Orono, Maine: University of Maine, 1967.

Lyle, J. G.   Certain antenatal, perinatal and developmental variables and reading retardation in middle-class boys. *Child Development*, 1970, *41*, 481–491.

Martin, C.   Developmental interrelationships among language variables in children of the first grade. *Elementary English*, 1955, *32*,
167–171.

Masland, M. W., and Case, L.   Limitation of auditory memory as a
factor in delayed language development. Paper read at the International Association for Logopedics and Phoniatrics, Vienna,
1965.

Masland, R. L.   Some neurological processes underlying language.
Annals of Otology, Rhinology and Laryngology, 1968, *77*, 787–
804.

McNeill, D.   *The Acquisition of Language: The Study of Developmental Psycholinguistics*. New York: Harper & Row, 1970.

Menyuk, P.   Comparison of grammar of children with functionally
deviant and normal speech. *Journal of Speech and Hearing Research*, 1964, *7*, 109–121.

Meyer, G.   Some relationships between Rorschach scores in kindergarten and reading in the primary grades. *Journal of Projective
Techniques*, 1953, *17*, 414–425.

Miller, W. H.   Relationship between mother's style of communication
and her control system to the child's reading readiness and subsequent reading achievement in first grade. Unpublished Ed.D. dissertation, University of Arizona, 1967.

Minuchin, P.   Correlates of curiosity and exploratory behavior in preschool disadvantaged children. *Child Development*, 1971, *42*,
939–950.

Moe, I. L.   Auding as a predictive measure of reading performance in
primary grades. Unpublished doctoral dissertation, University of
Florida, 1957.

Monroe, M.   Reading aptitude tests for prediction and analysis of
reading abilities and disabilities. Primary form. *Education*, 1935,
56, 7–14.

Montagu, A.   Sociogenic brain damage. *Developmental Medicine and
Child Neurology*, 1971, *13*, 597–605.

Morphett, M. V., and Washburne, C.   When should children begin to
read? *Elementary School Journal*, 1931, *31*, 496–503.

Muehl, S., and Kremenack, S.   Ability to match information within
and between auditory and visual sense modalities and subsequent
reading achievement. *Journal of Educational Psychology*, 1966,
57 (4), 230–239.

Muir, R. C., Lester, E. P., Dudek, S. Z., and Harris, B. R.   Cognition
and adaptation in the young child. *American Journal of Orthopsychiatry*, 1969, *39*, 240–241.

Neisser, U.   The processes of vision. *Scientific American*, 1968 (Sept.),
pp. 204–214.

Olson, A. V.   Growth in word perception abilities as it relates to success in beginning reading. *Journal of Education*, 1958, *140* (3), 25–36.

Orton, S. T. Familial occurrence of disorders in the acquisition of language. *Eugenics*, 1930, *3*, 140–147.

Orton, S. T. *Reading, Writing and Speech Problems in Children.* New York: W. W. Norton, 1937.

Piaget, J. *The Origins of Intelligence in Children.* New York: International Universities Press, 1952.

Piaget, J., and Inhelder, B. *The Growth of Logical Thinking from Childhood to Adolescence.* New York: Basic Books, 1958.

Robinson, H. M. Vocabulary: Speaking, listening, reading and writing. In H. A. Robinson (Ed.), *Reading and the Language Arts.* Chicago: University of Chicago Press, 1963.

Rosenthal, R., and Jacobson, L. *Pygmalion in the Classroom.* New York: Holt, Rinehart & Winston, 1968.

Ryan, E., and Semmel, M. Reading as a constructive language process. *Reading Research Quarterly*, 1969, *5* (1), 59–83.

Ryans, D. G. *Characteristics of Teachers.* Washington, D.C.: American Council on Education, 1960.

Schwartz, F., and Schiller, P. A psychoanalytical model of attention and learning. *Psychological Issues*, 1970, *6* (3). Monograph 23. New York: International Universities Press, 1970.

Shipps, D. E., and Loudon, M. L. The draw-a-man test and achievement in the first grade. *Journal of Educational Research*, 1964, *57*, 518–521.

Silvaroli, N. J. Factors in predicting children's success in first grade reading. In J. A. Figurel (Ed.), *Reading and Inquiry.* International Reading Association Conference Proceedings, Vol. 10. Newark, Del.: International Reading Association, 1965.

Silver, A., and Hagin, R. Specific reading disability: Delineation of the syndrome and relationship to cerebral dominance. *Comprehensive Psychiatry*, 1960, *1*, 126–134.

Simon, J. Une batterie d'épreuves psychologiques pour la prédiction de la réussite en lecture. *Enfance*, 1952, *5*, 457–480.

Singer, J., Westphal, M., and Niswander, K. R. Sex differences in the incidence of neonatal abnormalities and abnormal performance in early childhood. *Child Development*, 1968, *39* (1), 103–112.

Smith, F., and Holmes, D. L. The independence of letter, word and meaning identification in reading. *Reading Research Quarterly*, 1971, *6*, 394–415.

Smith, N. B. (Ed.). *Reading methods and teacher improvement.* Newark, Del.: International Reading Association, 1971.

Spache, G. D. A study of a longitudinal first grade reading readiness program. U.S. Office of Education Cooperative Research Project

No. 2747. Washington, D.C.: U.S. Department of Health, Education and Welfare, 1965.

Sperry, B., Staver, N., Reiner, B. S., and Ulrich, D.   Renunciation and denial in learning difficulties. *American Journal of Orthopsychiatry*, 1958, *28* (1), 98–111.

St. John, N.   Thirty-six teachers: Their characteristics and outcomes for black and white pupils. *American Educational Research Journal*, 1971, *8* (4), 635–648.

Stamback, M.   Le problème du rhythme dans le développement de l'enfant et dans les dyslexies d'évolution. *Enfance*, 1951, *4*, 480–502.

Stanchfield, J. M.   Development of pre-reading skills in an experimental kindergarten program. *Reading Teacher*, 1971, *24* (8), 699–707.

Stodolsky, S. S., and Lesser, G. S.   Learning patterns in the disadvantaged. *Harvard Educational Review*, 1967, *37*, 546–593.

Subirana, A.   The problem of cerebral dominance: The relationship between handedness and language function. *Logos*, 1961, *4*, 67–85.

Sutton, M. H.   Readiness for reading at the kindergarten level. *Reading Teacher*, 1964, *17*, 234–239.

Sutton, M. H.   Children who learned to read in kindergarten: A longitudinal study. *Reading Teacher*, 1969, *22*, 595–602, 683.

Tanner, J. M.   *Education and Physical Growth*. London: University of London Press, 1961.

Thomas, A., Chess, S., Birch, H. G., Hertzig, M. E., and Korn, S.   *Behavioral Individuality in Early Childhood*. New York: New York University Press, 1963.

Thorndike, R. L.   A review of "Pygmalion in the Classroom." *American Educational Research Journal*, 1968, *5*, 708–711.

Vygotsky, L. S.   *Thought and Language*. Cambridge, Mass.: M.I.T. Press, 1962.

Wattenberg, W. W., and Clifford, C.   Relationship of the self-concept to beginning achievement in reading. *Child Development*, 1964, *35* (1), 461–467.

Weber, R. M.   The study of oral reading errors: A survey of the literature. *Reading Research Quarterly*, 1968, *4*, 96–119.

Weiner, M., and Feldmann, S.   Validation studies of a reading prognosis test for children of lower and middle socio-economic status. *Educational and Psychological Measurement*, 1950, *23*, 807–814.

Weintraub, S.   What research says to the reading teacher: Readiness measures for predicting reading achievement. *Reading Teacher*, 1967, *20*, 551–558.

Weintraub, S.   Visual perceptual factors in reading. In M. M. Clark and S. M. Maxwell (Eds.), *Reading: Influences on Progress*. Pro-

ceedings of the Fifth Annual Study Congress of the United Kingdom Reading Association, Edinburgh, 1967–68.

Wiener, M., and Cromer, W.   Reading and reading difficulty: A conceptual analysis. *Harvard Educational Review*, 1967, *37*, 620–643.

2. A New Plan for Prediction

Blank, M., and Bridger, W.   Cross-modal transfer in nursery-school
children. *Journal of Comparative and Physiological Psychology*,
1964, *58*, 227–282.

Dykstra, R.   The use of reading readiness tests for prediction and
diagnosis: A critique. *Perspectives in Reading*, 1967, No. 8, 35–50.

Kagan, J.   Sesame Street getting high marks. *The New York Times*,
October 17, 1971, p. 68.

Piaget, J.   *Six Psychological Studies*. New York: Random House, 1967.

St. John, N.   Thirty-six teachers: Their characteristics and outcomes
for black and white pupils. *American Educational Research Journal*, 1971, *8* (4), 635–648.

3. Diagnosis

Bateman, B.   The role of individual diagnosis in remedial planning for
reading disorders. In E. O. Calkins (Ed.), *Reading Forum*, National
Institute of Neurological Disease and Stroke, Monograph No. 11,
1971, p. 127.

Leton, D.   A factor analysis of readiness tests. *Perceptual and Motor
Skills*, 1963, *16*, 915–919.

Lowell, R.   Selected reading readiness tests as predictors of success in
reading. U.S. Office of Education Project No. 6-8894. Orono,
Maine: University of Maine, 1967.

Mann, L.   Psychometric phrenology and the new faculty psychology:
The case against ability assessment and training. *Journal of Special
Education*, 1971, *5*, 3–13.

Meyers, C. E., Dingman, H. F., Orpet, R. E., Sitkei, E. G., and Watts,
C. A.   Four ability-factor hypotheses at three preliterate levels in
normal and retarded children. *Monographs of the Society for
Research in Child Development*, 1964, *29* (5) (whole No. 96),
1–80.

Olson, A.   Factor analytic study of the Frostig Developmental Test of
Visual Perception. *Journal of Special Education*, 1968, *2*, 429–
433.

Olson, A. and Fitzgibbon, N.   Factor analytic investigation of two
reading readiness tests. *Perceptual and Motor Skills*, 1968, *27*,
611–614.

Roswell, F., and Natchez, G. *Reading Disability: Diagnosis and Treatment.* New York: Basic Books, 1964.

Spache, G., Andres, M., Curtis, H. A., Rowland, M., and Fields, M. A longitudinal first grade reading readiness program. *Reading Teacher,* 1966, *19,* 580–584.

Thurstone, L. L., and Thurstone, T. SRA primary mental abilities: Technical report. Chicago: Science Research Associates, 1965.

Wiener, M. and Cromer, W. Reading and reading difficulty: A conceptual analysis. *Harvard Educational Review,* 1967, *37,* 620–643.

4. Reading Failure

Zedler, E. Development of competencies for the teaching of reading to children who have not learned under conventional procedures. In E. O. Calkins (Ed.), *Reading Forum,* National Institute of Neurological Disease and Stroke, Monograph No. 11, 1971, pp. 225–234.

5. Intervention

Anderson, R. W. Effects of neuro-psychological techniques on reading achievement. Unpublished doctoral dissertation, Colorado State College, 1965.

Asbed, R. A., Masland, M. W., Sever, J. L., and Weinberg, M. M. Early case finding of children with communication problems: Part I. Report of a community screening program. *Volta Review,* 1970, *72,* 23–50.

Ausubel, D. P. The effects of cultural deprivation on learning patterns. In S. W. Webster (Ed.), *Understanding the Educational Problems of the Disadvantaged Learner.* San Francisco: Chandler, 1966.

Baratz, S., and Baratz, J. Early childhood intervention: The social science base of institutional racism. *Harvard Educational Review,* 1970, *40* (1), 29–50.

Bennet, E. L., Diamond, M., Krech, D., and Rosenzweig, M. R. Chemical and anatomical plasticity of the brain. *Science,* 1964, *146,* 610–619.

Bereiter, C. Genetics and educability: Educational implications of the Jensen debate. In J. Hellmuth (Ed.), *Disadvantaged Child.* Vol. 3. New York: Brunner/Mazel, 1970.

Bereiter, C. and Engelmann, S. *Teaching Disadvantaged Children in the Preschool.* Englewood Cliffs, N.J.: Prentice-Hall, 1966.

Bibance, R., and Hancock, K. Relationships between perceptual and conceptual cognitive processes. *Journal of Learning Disabilities,* 1969, *2,* 17–29.

Biber, B.   Discussion of Ausubel's presentation. In P. B. Neubauer (Ed.), *Concepts of Development in Early Childhood Education.* Springfield, Ill.: Thomas, 1965.

Bing, E.   Effects of childrearing practices on development of differential cognitive abilities. *Child Development,* 1963, *34,* 631–648.

Birch, H. G.   Health and the education of socially disadvantaged children. *Developmental Medicine and Child Neurology,* 1968, *10,* 580–599.

Birch, H. G.   Research issues in child health: IV. Some philosophic and methodologic issues. In E. Grotberg (Ed.), *Critical Issues in Research Related to Disadvantaged Children.* Princeton, N.J.: Educational Testing Service, 1969.

Birch, H. G.   Research issues in child health: Some philosophic and methodologic issues. *Pediatrics,* 1970, *45* (5), 874–883.

Blank, M. A.   A methodology for fostering abstract thinking in deprived children. Paper presented at Ontario Institute for Studies in Education Conference on "Problems in the Teaching of Young Children," Toronto, March 1968.

Blodgett, E. G., and Cooper, E. B.   Attitudes of elementary school teachers toward black dialect. Paper presented at American Speech and Hearing Association convention, Chicago, September 1971.

Bloom, B. S.   *Stability and Change in Human Characteristics.* New York: Wiley, 1964.

Brottman, M. A. (Ed.).   *Language Remediation for the Disadvantaged Preschool Child.* Society for Research in Child Development Monographs, Serial No. 124, 1968, *33* (8).

Bruner, J. S.   *The Process of Education.* Cambridge, Mass.: Harvard University Press, 1963.

Buktenica, N. A.   Perceptual mode dominance: An approach to assessment of first-grade reading and spelling. In *Proceedings, 76th Annual Convention, American Psychological Association.* Washington, D.C., APA, 1968.

Caldwell, B. M.   What is the optimal learning environment for the young child? In S. Chess and A. Thomas (Eds.), *Annual Progress in Child Psychiatry and Child Development, 1968.* New York: Brunner/Mazel, 1968.

Caldwell, B. M.   The effects of psychosocial deprivation on human development in infancy. In S. Chess and A. Thomas (Eds.), *Annual Progress in Child Psychiatry and Child Development, 1971.* New York: Brunner/Mazel, 1971.

Cawley, J. F.   Components of a system of initial reading instruction. In N. G. Haring (Ed.), *Instructional Improvement: Behavior*

Modification. Workshop book from the Child Study and Treatment Center, Fort Steilacoom, Wash., June 1968.

Cazden, C. B.   The situation: A neglected source of social class differences in language use. *Journal of Social Issues,* 1970, *26* (2), 35–60.

Cazden, C. B.   Evaluation of learning in preschool education: Early language development. In B. Bloom, T. Hastings, and G. Madaus (Eds.), *Formative and Summative Evaluation of Student Learning.* New York: McGraw-Hill, 1971.

Cazden, C. B., Baratz, J. C., Labov, W., and Palmer, F. H.   Language development in day-care programs. Office of Economic Opportunity, October 1970. Mimeo.

Chansky, N. M., and Taylor, M.   Perceptual training with young mental retardates. *American Journal of Mental Deficiency,* 1964, *68,* 460–468.

Child Development Task Force.   *Child Development: Summary of the Child Development Task Force Report.* Washington, D.C.: U. S. Department of Health, Education and Welfare, April 1968.

Cohen, S. A.   Studies in visual perception and reading in disadvantaged children. *Journal of Learning Disabilities,* 1969, *2,* 498–507.

Coleman, J. S., Campbell, G. Q., Hobson, C. J., McPartland, J., Mood, A. M., Weinfeld, F. D., York, R. L.   *Equality of Educational Opportunity.* Report of the U.S. Department of Health, Education and Welfare, Washington, D.C.: U.S. Government Printing Office, 1966.

Crandall, V. J., Preston, A., and Rabson, A.   Maternal relations and the development of independence and achievement behavior in young children. *Child Development,* 1960, *31,* 243–251.

Cravioto, J., and Robles, B.   Evolution of adaptive and motor behavior during rehabilitation from kwashiorkor. *American Journal of Orthopsychiatry,* 1965, *35* (3), 449–464.

Crawford, C. H.   A family day care program. In W. G. Hardy (Ed.), *Communication and the Disadvantaged Child.* Baltimore: Williams & Wilkins, 1970.

D'Amato, M. R., and Jagoda, H.   Effect of early exposure to photic stimulation on brightness discrimination and exploratory behavior. *Journal of Genetic Psychology,* 1962, *101* (2), 267–271.

de Hirsch, K., Jansky, J. J., and Langford, W. S.   *Predicting Reading Failure.* New York: Harper & Row, 1966.

Delacato, C. H.   *Neurological Organization and Reading.* Springfield, Ill.: Thomas, 1966.

Deutsch, M.   *Annual Report: Institute for Developmental Studies.* New York: New York University, 1965a.

Deutsch, M.   The role of social class in language development and cognition. *American Journal of Orthopsychiatry,* 1965b, *35,* 78–88.

Deutsch, M.   *The Disadvantaged Child: Studies of the Social Environment and the Learning Process.* New York: Basic Books, 1967.

Deutsch, M., and Brown, B.   Social influences in Negro-white intelligence differences. *Journal of Social Issues,* 1964, *20* (2), 24–35.

Diagnostically Based Curriculum, Bloomington, Indiana. U.S. Department of Health, Education and Welfare Pamphlet, No. OE-37024. Washington, D.C.: U.S. Government Printing Office, 1967.

Dickie, J. P.   Effectiveness of structured and unstructured (traditional) methods of language training. In M. Brottman (Ed.), *Language Remediation for the Disadvantaged Preschool Child.* Society for Research in Child Development Monographs, Serial No. 124, 1968, *33* (8).

Eckstein, R., and Motto, R. L.   *From Learning for Love to Love of Learning.* New York: Brunner/Mazel, 1969.

Engelmann, S.   The effectiveness of direct instruction on IQ performance and achievement in reading and arithmetic. In J. Hellmuth (Ed.), *Disadvantaged Child,* Vol. 3. New York: Brunner/Mazel, 1970.

Feldmann, S. C., Schmidt, D. E., and Deutsch, C. P.   Effect of auditory training on reading skills of retarded readers. *Perceptual and Motor Skills,* 1968, *26,* 467–480.

Flavell, J., and Hill, J.   Developmental psychology. *Annual Review of Psychology,* 1969, *20,* 1–56.

Flavell, J., and Wohlwill, J.   Formal and functional aspects of cognitive development. In D. Elkind and J. Flavell (Eds.), *Studies in Cognitive Development.* New York: Oxford University Press, 1969.

Freud, A.   *Normality and Pathology in Childhood.* New York: International Universities Press, 1965.

Friedlander, B. Z.   The effect of speaker identity, voice inflection, vocabulary and message redundancy on infants' selection of vocal reinforcement. *Journal of Experimental Child Psychology,* 1968, *6,* 443–459.

Gibson, E. J.   Perceptual learning in educational situations. Paper for the Symposium in the Research Approach to the Learning of School Subjects, Cornell, 1966. Mimeo.

Gleason, J. B.   Do children imitate? *Proceedings of the International Conference on Oral Education of the Deaf,* 1967, *2,* 1441–1448.

Goldfarb, W.   Psychological privation in infancy and subsequent adjustment. *American Journal of Orthopsychiatry,* 1945, *15* (2), 247–255.

Goodman, K. S.   Reading: The key is in children's language. *Reading Teacher,* 1972, *25* (6), 505–508.

Haggerty, R. J.   Research issues in child health: II. Some medical and economic issues. In E. Grotberg (Ed.), *Critical Issues in Research Related to Disadvantaged Children*. Princeton, N.J.: Educational Testing Service, 1969.

Hebb, D. O.   *The Organization of Behavior.* New York: Wiley, 1949.

Heber, R., and Garber, H.   An experiment in the prevention of cultural-familial mental retardation. Paper presented at the proceedings of the Second Congress of the International Association for the Scientific Study of Mental Deficiency, Warsaw, Poland, 1970.

Held, R., and Freedman, S. J.   Plasticity in human sensorimotor control. *Science*, 1963, *142* (3591), 455–462.

Hertzig, M. E., and Birch, H. G.   Longitudinal course of measured intelligence in preschool children of different social and ethnic backgrounds. *American Journal of Orthopsychiatry*, 1971, *41* (3), 416–426.

Hertzig, M. E., Birch, H. G., Thomas, A., and Mendez, O. A.   *Class and Ethnic Differences in the Responsiveness of Preschool Children to Cognitive Demands.* Society for Research in Child Development Monographs, Serial No. 117, 1968, *33* (1).

Hess, R. D.   Early education as socialization. In R. D. Hess and R. M. Bear (Eds.), *Early Education: Current Theory, Research and Action.* Chicago: Aldine, 1966.

Holmes, J., and Singer, H.   *The Substrata-Factor Theory: Substrata Differences Underlying Reading Ability in Known Groups.* Washington, D.C.: U.S. Office of Education, 1961.

Horn, R. D.   Three methods of developing reading readiness in Spanish-speaking children in first grade. *Reading Teacher*, 1966, *19*, 38–42.

Horn, T. D. (Ed.).   *Reading for the Disadvantaged: Problems of Linguistically Different Learners.* New York: Harcourt, Brace & World, 1970.

Horner, V. and John, V.   Bilingualism and the Spanish-speaking child. In F. Williams (Ed.), *Language and Poverty: Perspectives on a Theme.* Chicago: Markham, 1970.

Houston, S. H.   A re-examination of some assumptions about the language of the disadvantaged child. *Child Development*, 1970, *41* (4), 947–963.

Hunt, J. McV.   *Intelligence and Experience.* New York: Ronald Press, 1961.

Hunt, J. McV.   The psychological basis for using preschool enrichment as an antidote for cultural deprivation. *Merrill-Palmer Quarterly*, 1964, *10*, 309–348.

Irwin, O. C.   Infant speech: Effect of systematic reading of stories. *Journal of Speech and Hearing Research*, 1960, *3*, 187–190.

Isaacs, S.   *Intellectual Growth in Young Children.* London: Routledge, 1930.

Jackson, P. W. *The Teacher and the Machine.* Pittsburgh: University of Pittsburgh Press, 1968.

Jeruchimowicz, R., Costello, J., and Bagur, J. S. Knowledge of action and object words: A comparison of lower and middle-class Negro preschoolers. *Child Development,* 1971, *42* (2), 455–464.

Kagan, J. Continuity in cognitive development during the first year. *Merrill-Palmer Quarterly,* 1969a, *15,* 101–120.

Kagan, J. Personality and intellectual development in the school-age child. In I. Janis (Ed.), *Personality: Dynamics, Development and Assessment.* New York: Harcourt, Brace & World, 1969b.

Kappelman, M. M., Kaplan, E., and Ganter, R. L. A study of learning disorders among disadvantaged children. In S. Chess and A. Thomas (Eds.), *Annual Progress in Child Psychiatry and Child Development, 1970.* New York: Brunner/Mazel, 1970.

Karnes, M. B., Hodgins, A. S., Stoneburner, R. L., Studley, W. M., and Toska, J. A. Effects of a highly structured program of language development on intellectual functioning and psycholinguistic development of culturally disadvantaged three-year-olds. *Journal of Special Education,* 1969, *2* (4), 405–413.

Karnes, M. B., Studley, W. M., Wright, W. R., and Hodgins, A. S. An approach for working with mothers of disadvantaged preschool children. *Merrill-Palmer Quarterly,* 1968, *14* (2), 173–184.

Kass, W. Learning problems, neurological deficit and school forceout. Workshop paper presented at the American Orthopsychiatric Association Meeting, New York, March 1969.

Kephart, N. C. *The Slow Learner in the Classroom.* Columbus, Ohio: Merrill, 1960.

Kimura, D. Cerebral dominance and the perception of verbal stimuli. *Canadian Journal of Psychology,* 1961, *15,* 166–171.

Klaus, R. A., and Gray, S. W. *The Early Training Project for Disadvantaged Children: A Report After Five Years.* Society for Research in Child Development Monographs, Serial No. 120, 1968, *33* (4).

Kofsky, E. The effect of verbal training on concept identification in disadvantaged children. *Psychonomic Science,* 1967, *7,* 356–366.

Kohlberg, L. Early education: A cognitive-developmental view. *Child Development,* 1968, *39,* 1013–1062.

Kolers, P. A. Reading is only incidentally visual. In K. Goodman and J. Fleming (Eds.), *Psycholinguistics and the Teaching of Reading.* Newark, Del.: International Reading Association, 1969.

Labov, W. Some sources of reading problems for Negro speakers of non-standard English. In A. Frazier (Ed.), *New Directions in Elementary English.* Champaign, Ill.: National Council of Teachers of English, 1967.

Labov, W. The logic of non-standard dialect. In *Georgetown Mono-*

graph Series on Language and Linguistics, Monograph No. 22, 1969, 1–43.

Lally, J. R.   Syracuse University Children's Center: A Day Care Center for Young Children. Syracuse University, February 1970. Mimeo.

Lambie, D. Z., and Weikert, D. P.   Ypsilanti Carnegie Infant Education Project. In J. Hellmuth (Ed.), *Disadvantaged Child*. Vol. 3. New York: Brunner/Mazel, 1970.

Lawton, D.   *Social Class, Language and Education*. New York: Schocken, 1968.

Lenneberg, E. H.   *Biological Foundations of Language*. New York: Wiley, 1967.

LeShan, L. L.   Time orientation and social class. *Journal of Abnormal and Social Psychology*, 1952, *47*, 589–592.

Levenstein, P.   Cognitive growth in preschoolers through stimulation of verbal interaction with mothers. *American Journal of Orthopsychiatry*, 1969, *39*, (2), 239–240.

Liberman, I. Y.   Speech and lateralization of language. *Bulletin of the Orton Soceity*, 1971, *21*, 71–86.

Light, R., and Smith, P.   Choosing a future: Strategies for designing and evaluating new programs. *Harvard Educational Review*, 1970, *40* (1), 1–28.

Lumsdaine, A. A.   Assessing the effectiveness of instructional programs. In A. A. Lumsdaine and R. Glaser (Eds.), *Teaching Machines and Programmed Learning II*. Washington, D. C.: Department of Audio-Visual Instruction, National Education Association, 1961.

Luria, A. R.   *The Role of Speech in the Regulation of Normal and Abnormal Behavior*. London: Pergamon Press, 1961.

Lustman, S. L.   Cultural deprivation: A clinical dimension of education. *The Psychoanalytic Study of the Child*, 1970, *XXV*. New York: International Universities Press, 1970.

Mann, L.   Perceptual training: Misdirections and redirections. Unpublished paper, Office of the County Superintendent of Schools, Montgomery County, Pa., 1968.

Marans, A. E., and Lourie, R.   Hypotheses regarding the effects of childrearing patterns on the disadvantaged child. In J. Hellmuth (Ed.), *Disadvantaged Child*, Vol. 1. New York: Brunner/Mazel, 1967.

Masland, M. W.   Personal communication, 1971.

Masland, R.   The nature of the reading process: The rationale of non-educational remedial methods. College of Physicians and Surgeons, Columbia University, 1969. Mimeo.

Masland, R., and Cratty, B. J.   The nature of the reading process, the rationale of non-educational remedial methods. In E. O. Calkins

(Ed.), *Reading Forum: A Collection of Reference Papers Concerned with Reading Disability.* National Institute of Neurological Disease and Stroke, Monograph No. 11. Washington, D. C.: U.S. Government Printing Office, 1971.

Mason, A. W.   Follow-up of educational attainments in a group of children with retarded speech development and in a control group. In M. Clark and S. Maxwell (Eds.), *Reading: Influences on Progress.* Proceedings of the Fifth Annual Study Congress of the United Kingdom Reading Association, Edinburgh, 1967–68.

Maynard, J. C.   Day care programs: A mandate for change. In W. G. Hardy (Ed.), *Communication and the Disadvantaged Child.* Baltimore: Williams & Wilkins, 1970.

Meers, D. R.   Contributions of a ghetto culture to symptom formation: Psychoanalytic studies of ego anomalies in Negro childhood. *American Journal of Orthopsychiatry,* 1969, *39* (2), 278–279.

Milner, E. A.   A study of the relationships between reading readiness in grade one school children and patterns of parent-child interaction. *Child Development,* 1951, *22,* 95–122.

Minuchin, P., and Biber, B.   A child development approach to language in the disadvantaged preschool child. In M. Brottman (Ed.), *Language Remediation for the Disadvantaged Child.* Society for Research in Child Development Monographs, Serial No. 124, 1968, *33* (8).

Moskovitz, S. T.   Some assumptions underlying the Bereiter approach. *Young Children,* 1968, *23,* 24–31.

Olson, A.   Factor analytic study of the Frostig Developmental Test of Visual Perception. *Journal of Special Education,* 1968, *2,* 429–433.

Palmer, F. H.   Early intellective training and school performance. Unpublished paper, City University of New York, 1968.

Paraprofessionals learn to identify problem readers early. *Report on Educational Research,* Sept. 29, 1971, p. 10.

Pasamanick, B.   A tract for the times: Some sociobiologic aspects of science, race and racism. *American Journal of Orthopsychiatry,* 1969, *39,* 7–15.

Pasamanick, B., and Knobloch, H.   The contribution of some organic factors to school retardation in Negro children. *Journal of Negro Education,* 1958, *27,* 4–9.

Penfield, W., and Roberts, L.   *Speech and Brain Mechanisms.* Princeton, N.J.: Princeton University Press, 1959.

Perry Preschool Project, Ypsilanti, Michigan. U.S. Department of Health, Education and Welfare Pamphlet No. OE-37035. Washington: U.S. Government Printing Office, 1967.

Piaget, J.   *The Origins of Intelligence in Children.* New York: International Universities Press, 1952.

Piaget, J.   *Thinking and Speaking: A Symposium.* Amsterdam: North Holland Publishing Co., 1954.

Pines, M.   Why some 3-year-olds get A's—and some get C's. *New York Times Magazine,* July 6, 1969, pp. 4–17.

Pollack, R. H.   Some implications of ontogenetic changes in perception. In D. Elkind and J. Flavell (Eds.), *Studies in Cognitive Development.* New York: Oxford University Press, 1969.

Provence, S., and Lipton, R.   *Infants in Institutions.* New York: International Universities Press, 1962.

Radin, N.   The impact of a kindergarten home counseling program. *Exceptional Children,* 1969, *36* (4), 251–256.

Riesen, A. H.   Stimulation as a requirement for growth and function in behavioral development. In D. Fiske and S. Maddi (Eds.), *Functions of Varied Experience.* Homewood, Ill.: Dorsey Press, 1961.

Rosen, C. L., and Ortego, P. D. (Eds.).   *Issues in Language and Reading Instruction of Spanish-Speaking Children.* Newark, Del.: International Reading Association, 1969.

Rutherford, W.   Perceptual-motor training and readiness. Paper presented at the Tenth Annual Conference of the International Reading Association, Detroit, May 1965.

Ryan, E., and Semmel, M.   Reading as a constructive language process. *Reading Research Quarterly,* 1969, *5* (1), 59–83.

Schaefer, E. S.   Intellectual stimulation of culturally deprived infants. Unpublished progress report, National Institutes of Mental Health, 1965.

Schaefer, E. S.   Home tutoring, maternal behavior and infant intellectual development. Paper delivered at the American Psychological Association, Washington, D.C., 1969.

Scheinfeld, D., Bowles, D., Tuck, S., and Gold, R.   Parents' values, family networks and family development: Working and disadvantaged families. *American Journal of Orthopsychiatry,* 1970, *40* (3), 413–425.

Schiff, S. K.   New look at children's potential: Results of a six-year community-wide mental health program for over 10,000 children. *American Journal of Orthopsychiatry,* 1971, *41* (2), 322–323.

Schilder, P.   *Contributions to Developmental Neuropsychiatry.* New York: International Universities Press, 1964.

Scott, J. P.   Critical periods in behavior development. *Science,* 1962, 138, 949–958.

Scrimshaw, N. S.   Early malnutrition and central nervous system function. In S. Chess and A. Thomas (Eds.), *Annual Progress in Child Psychiatry and Child Development, 1970.* New York: Brunner/Mazel, 1970.

Slaughter, D. T.   Parental potency and the achievements of inner-city black children. *American Journal of Orthopsychiatry,* 1970, *40* (3), 433–440.

Stanchfield, J. M.   Development of pre-reading skills in an experimental kindergarten program. *Reading Teacher,* 1971, *24* (8), 699–707.

Stern, C.   Evaluating language curricula for preschool children. In M. Brottman (Ed.), *Language Remediation for the Disadvantaged Preschool Child.* Society for Research in Child Development Monographs, Serial No. 124, 1968, *33* (8), 49–61.

Stone, M., and Pielstick, N. L.   Effectiveness of Delacato treatment with kindergarten children. *Psychology in the Schools,* 1969, *6,* 63–68.

Swift, M. S.   Training poverty mothers in communication skills. *Reading Teacher,* 1970, *23* (4), 360–367.

Tannenbaum, J. A.   Developmental scores on Children's Center graduates. Syracuse University, 1970. Mimeo.

Taylor, T.   Experiences with a day care program. In W. G. Hardy (Ed.), *Communication and the Disadvantaged Child.* Baltimore: Williams & Wilkins, 1970.

Thomas, A., Hertzig, M. E., Dryman, I., and Fernandez, P.   Examiner effect in IQ testing of Puerto Rican working-class children. *American Journal of Orthopsychiatry,* 1971, *41* (5), 809–821.

Vygotsky, L. S.   *Thought and Language.* Cambridge, Mass.: M.I.T. Press, 1962.

Weikert, D. P., Deloria, D. J., Lawser, S. A., and Weigerink, R.   *Longitudinal Results of the Ypsilanti Perry Preschool Project.* Ypsilanti, Mich.: High/Scope Educational Research Foundation, 1970.

Weikert, D. P., and Lambie, D. Z.   Preschool intervention through a home teaching program. In J. Hellmuth (Ed.), *Disadvantaged Child,* Vol. 2. New York: Brunner/Mazel, 1968.

Weintraub, S., Robinson, H. M., Smith, H. K., and Plessas, G. P.   Summary of investigations relating to reading, July 1, 1969, to June 30, 1970. *Reading Research Quarterly,* 1971, *6,* 137–319.

Werner, H.   The concept of development from a comparative and organismic point of view. In D. B. Harris (Ed.), *The Concept of Development.* Minneapolis: University of Minnesota Press, 1957.

White, B. L.   An experimental approach to the effects of experience on early human behavior. In J. P. Hill (Ed.), *Minnesota Symposia on Child Psychology,* Vol. 1. Minneapolis: University of Minnesota Press, 1967.

Winsberg, B. G.   Programmed learning, teaching machines and dyslexia. *American Journal of Orthopsychiatry,* 1969, *39,* 418–427.

Wolf, R.   The measurement of environment. In W. MacGinitie and S.

Ball (Eds.), *Readings in the Psychological Foundations of Education.* New York: McGraw-Hill, 1968.

Wortis, H., Bardach, J. L., Cutler, R., Rue, R., and Freedman, A. Childrearing practices in a low socioeconomic group: The mothers of premature infants. *Pediatrics,* 1963, *32,* 298–307.

Wyatt, G. L.   *Language Learning and Communication Disorders in Children.* New York: Free Press, 1969.

Zimiles, H.   An analysis of current issues in the evaluation of educational programs. In J. Hellmuth (Ed.), *Disadvantaged Child.* Vol. 2. New York: Brunner/Mazel, 1968.

Zimiles, H.   Has evaluation failed compensatory education? In J. Hellmuth (Ed.), *Disadvantaged Child.* Vol. 3. New York: Brunner/Mazel, 1970.

Zintz, M. V.   Cultural aspects of bilingualism. In P. S. Anderson (Ed.), *Linguistics in the Elementary School Classroom.* New York: Macmillan, 1971.

Index